MORE 'INSTRUCTIONS FROM THE CENTRE': TOP SECRET FILES ON KGB GLOBAL OPERATIONS, 1975–1985

By Christopher Andrew and Oleg Gordievsky

*KGB: The Inside Story of its Foreign Operations from
Lenin to Gorbachev*
(Hodder & Stoughton, 1990)

*Instructions From The Centre:
Top Secret Files on KGB Global Operations, 1975–1985*
(Hodder & Stoughton, 1991)

By Christopher Andrew

Théophile Delcassé and the Making of the Entente Cordiale
(Macmillan, 1968)

The First World War: Causes and Consequences
(Volume 19 of the Hamlyn History of the World, 1970)

*France Overseas: The Great War and the Climax of French
Imperial Expansion*
With A.S. Kanya-Forstner
(Thames & Hudson, 1981)

*The Missing Dimension: Governments and Intelligence
Communities in the Twentieth Century*
With David Dilks (Macmillan, 1984)

*Secret Service: The Making of the British
Intelligence Community*
(Heinemann, 1985)

Codebreaking and Signals Intelligence
(Frank Cass, 1986)

Intelligence and International Relations, 1900–1945
With Jeremy Noakes
(Exeter University Press, 1987)

More
'Instructions from the Centre'

Top Secret Files on KGB Global Operations 1975–1985

EDITED BY

CHRISTOPHER ANDREW

AND

OLEG GORDIEVSKY

FRANK CASS

First published in 1992 in Great Britain by
FRANK CASS & CO. LTD.
Gainsborough House, Gainsborough Road,
London E11 1RS, England

and in the United States of America by
FRANK CASS
c/o International Specialized Book Services, Inc.
5602 N.E. Hassalo Street
Portland, Oregon 97213

Copyright © 1992 Frank Cass & Co. Ltd.

British Library Cataloguing in Publication Data

More Instructions from the Centre:Top
Secret Files on KGB Global Operations,
1975–85
I. Andrew, Christopher M.
II. Gordievsky, Oleg
327.1247

ISBN 0-7146-3475-1

Library of Congress Cataloging-in-Publication Data
More 'instructions from the centre' : top secret files on KGB global operations,
1975–1985 / edited by Christopher Andrew and Oleg
Gordievsky.
    p.   cm.
"First published as a special issue of the journal Intelligence and national
security, vol. 7, no. 1 (January 1992)"—T.p. verso.
ISBN 0-7146-3475-1 :
    1. Soviet Union. Komitet gosudarstvennoi bezopasnosti—History.
2. Intelligence service—Soviet Union—History.   I. Andrew,
Christopher M. II. Gordievsky, Oleg. III. Intelligence and
national security.
JN6529.I6M67   1992
    327.1'247'09—dc20   91-34825
                                                            CIP

Typeset by Regent Typesetting, London
Printed in Great Britain by
Antony Rowe Ltd, Chippenham, Wiltshire

Contents

Foreword

This volume contains a further selection of the highly classified KGB documents copied or photocopied by Oleg Gordievsky while serving as a PR line (political intelligence) officer in Copenhagen and London during the decade that culminated in the rise to power of Mikhail Sergeevich Gorbachev in 1985. The commentary has been written by Christopher Andrew, based on joint analysis of the documents with Oleg Gordievsky. We are very grateful to Dr Richard Popplewell for help with the translation of the documents.

This is a companion volume to our books, *KGB: The Inside Story of its Foreign Operations from Lenin to Gorbachev* (Hodder & Stoughton, 1990) and *Instructions from the Centre: Top Secret Files on KGB Foreign Operations, 1975–1985* (Hodder & Stoughton, 1991).

Abbreviations

A	Active Measures
ALP	Albanian Labour [Communist] Party
ANC	African National Congress
ARE	Arab Republic of Egypt
Centre	KGB Headquarters
CI	Counter-Intelligence
CIA	Central Intelligence Agency [USA]
CSCE	Conference on Security and Co-operation in Europe
DIA	Defence Intelligence Agency [USA]
DLB	Dead Letter-Box
DM	Documentary Material [KGB]
EEC	European Economic Community
FDC	KGB First Chief [Foreign Intelligence] Directorate
FRELIMO	Front for the Liberation of Mozambique
FRG	Federal Republic of Germany
GCHQ	Government Communications Headquarters [UK]
GRU	Soviet Military Intelligence
HVA	East German foreign intelligence agency
ICMB	Inter-Continental Ballistic Missile
K Directorate	FDC Counter-Intelligence Directorate
K Line	Operations against PRC in KGB Residencies
KGB	Committee of State Security
KR Line	Counter-Intelligence Department in KGB Residencies
MFA	Ministry of Foreign Affairs

N Line	Illegal Support Department in KGB Residencies
NATO	North Atlantic Treaty Organization
NSA	National Security Agency [USA]
OT	Operational-Technical [KGB]
PN	Undeveloped Negative [KGB]
PR Line	Political Intelligence Department in KGB Residencies
PRC	People's Republic of China
RYAN	Nuclear Missile Attack [KGB Operation]
S	*Spez*/Special
S Directorate	FDC Illegals Directorate
SIS	Secret Intelligence Service (UK)
Sigint	Intelligence derived from intercepting, decrypting and analysing signals
Sotsintern	Socialist International
SS	Special Secretariat (FDC)
S & T	Scientific and Technical/Technological Intelligence
SW	Secret Writing
SWAPO	South West Africa People's Organization
UNITA	Union for the Total Liberation of Angola
UZTS	Secure cipher room in Soviet mission
WJC	World Jewish Congress
WZO	World Zionist Organization
X Line	S & T Department in KGB Residencies
Z apparatus	Bugging and surveillance equipment [KGB]

KGB Codenames of Centre Officers and Residents

ALEKSEEV	Viktor Fyodorovich GRUSHKO (as Deputy Head, FCD)
ALYOSHIN	Vladimir Aleksandrovich KRYUCHKOV
GORNOV	Oleg Antonovich GORDIEVSKY
IRTYSHOV	Yevgeni Izotovich SHISHKIN
KORIN	Mikhail Petrovich LYUBIMOV
LAVROV	Leonid Yefremovich NIKITENKO
LEONOV	Leonid Yefremovich NIKITENKO
SEVEROV	Viktor Fyodorovich GRUSHKO (as Head of FCD Third Department)
SILIN	Gennadi Fyodorovich TITOV
SVETLOV	Nikolai Petrovich GRIBIN (not to be confused with 'Svetlov' at London Residency)
SVIRIDOV	Yuri Vladimirovich ANDROPOV
SVITOV	unidentified
VADIMOV	Vadim Vasilyevich KIRPICHENKO
VLADIMIROV	Anatoli Tikhonovich KIREEV
YERMAKOV	Arkadi Vasilyevich GUK

Notes: MS codenames written on documents by the Resident refer to Residency officers on the circulation list.

Format of KGB Communications from the Centre to Residencies

vn¹–1²

No. 1234³/PR⁴

Top Secret
To Residents

vn^1–1^2

No. 1234^3/PR^4

Top Secret

To Residents

We are sending you instructions on the work of sections of the Service and organizations abroad in 1984.

Attachment: As indicated in text, no. 1235/PR^5, Top Secret,
10 pages, PN^6
SILIN^7

Manuscript notes: Comr[ade] Gornov^8
Comr[ade] Fred^8
Comr[ade] Brown^8

Yermakov^9
14.12.83

KEY:

1 Initials of typist
2 Copy number (1 in this instance)
3 Number of despatch
4 Residency Line concerned (political intelligence in this instance)
5 Number and Line of enclosure
6 Format of enclosure (undeveloped film negative in this instance)
7 Codename of Centre officer signing despatch (G.F. Titov, head of FCD Third Department)
8 Codenames of Residency officers chosen by Resident to read despatch
9 Codename of Resident (A.V. Guk)

The United States: The 'Main Adversary'

From the end of the Second World War until the collapse of the Soviet system in 1991, the United States was the chief target (in KGB jargon 'The Main Adversary') of Soviet foreign intelligence. During the early years of Ronald Reagan's presidency, the Centre's fear of the Main Adversary was greater than at any time since the Cuban Missile Crisis of 1962. In 1981 the KGB began running jointly with the GRU its largest ever peacetime operation, codenamed RYAN, with the impossible objective of discovering the (non-existent) preparations by the United States and its NATO allies for a nuclear first strike against the Soviet Union.[1]

Though Operation RYAN wound down during 1984, the head of the FCD, Vladimir Aleksandrovich Kryuchkov (later Chairman of the KGB and one of the chief plotters in the abortive coup of August 1991), continued to insist on 'the especial importance of work on the USA in the present situation'. From 31 May 1984 Residencies around the world were ordered to send general reports every six months on their operations against the Main Adversary. Within the Centre these operations were co-ordinated by a section known as Group North, founded a decade earlier. Each Residency possessed a 'Main Adversary Group' consisting, typically, of one or two officers from the PR (political intelligence) and KR (counter-intelligence) lines, and one from Line X (scientific and technological intelligence) under a Line PR chairman. 'Group North' officers from the Centre made occasional visits to Residencies to inspect the work of Main Adversary Groups.

Kryuchkov was dissatisfied with the results achieved. In June 1984 he informed Residencies that 'all the diverse intelligence assignments against the USA' could not succeed unless there was a 'radical improvement' in agent recruitment:

N. 388
Top Secret
Copy No 1
[Ms notes:]
Comr Gornov
" Brown
" Artyom
and residency operational
staff
Lavrov [Nikitenko] 11.VII.84

No. 1095/PR/57
21.6.84
[Ms.] Gordon 17.7   [Ms.] Astakhov 17.7

OPERATIONAL REPORTING ON THE USA

The deterioration in the international situation and the growing immediate threat of war on the part of the United States mean that our Service is confronted ever more urgently with the task of operating against the USA as the main adversary. All the diverse intelligence assignments against the USA with which our service is faced have one factor in common: it is only possible to deal with them properly according to present-day standards if we have an effective agent organization operating in the principal American targets. Therefore the main criterion of efficiency in our apparatus abroad working against the USA must be its recruiting activity.

In recent years we have taken a number of steps designed to increase efficiency in recruitment work against the USA. This has enabled certain of our organizations abroad to achieve some solid results. Nevertheless, the general situation in the recruitment of Americans does not yet meet the requirements of our tasks and needs radical improvement.

In view of the especial degree of importance of work on the USA in the present situation, the new schedule for operational reporting which came into operation wef 31 May 1984, lays down that all stations abroad will report on their work on the USA twice a year (this procedure was formerly in force only for certain stations). In this context the requirements regarding the content of these reports acquire a high degree of importance.

The 'North' ['Sever'] group systematically analyses the reports from stations abroad passed to Centre about work against the USA. The information available provides evidence that the increased attention devoted to the question of operational reporting has in some measure been responsible for a number of stations abroad stepping up their work on the USA, and for more energetic checking of this work in the sections concerned in the Centre.

At the same time, operational reporting has not, up to now, become an effective means of improving the efficiency of our recruitment work against the USA. The majority of reports lack specific content, deal with questions of secondary importance and do not provide a complete picture of the activity of Residencies studying American targets. The following are among the most widespread shortcomings:

- a considerable amount of space is taken up in these reports by description of the agent/operational situation which is as a rule sufficiently well known to the section concerned in the Centre;
- in a number of reports, information-gathering is promoted to first place. This is typical of those Residencies where really systematic work is not being done to create agent bases in American targets;
- irrespective of the fact that the reports are supposed to be devoted to work on the USA, many stations include in them information about work on representatives of NATO countries and other sectors;
- many reports do not contain a critical analysis of the work done or an assessment of the results, nor do they contain information about implementation of the measures figuring in the Residency's work plan; they do not show evidence of a specific contribution from each officer;
- among the shortcomings is the related fact that reports are compiled in an arbitrary fashion and do not have a precisely defined structure. This makes it difficult to compare the results of the work or assess the effectiveness of the action taken.

We should like to emphasize firmly that the Centre understands very well the full complexity of the task of agent penetration of American targets and the extremely difficult conditions in which, at times, it has to be carried out. Therefore it is especially important that reporting should not be just for show purposes or stress the secondary aspects or formal side of the work, but should provide a genuine picture of how the real issue is being dealt with – i.e. cultivating and recruiting

Americans, how the agent apparatus is being created and used for this purpose, and what contribution each intelligence officer has made in the matter.

In sending these recommendations on compiling reports on work against the USA, we would draw the attention of heads of stations abroad to the fact that they bear personal responsibility for organizing work in this most important sector. We express a firm conviction that the operational staff of Residencies thoroughly understand the tasks arising out of the present complex international situation and will bend all their efforts to carrying out their duty to the Party and the service.

Attachment: Recommendations for compiling reports, No 1096/PR/ 57, three pages, secret, PN

ALYOSHIN
[KRYUCHKOV]
[Head of the FCD]

Secret
Copy No 1
Attachment to No. 1095/PR/57 of
21.06.84

Recommendations for compiling a report on work against the USA

A report on work directed against the USA must be presented as a consolidated document about the work done by the station on agent penetration into American targets. It should not be more than 3–4 pages in length and should set out in concise form the results of the Residency's work in this sector during the period under review.

The report should contain information about progress in dealing with the points in the plans for this part of the Residency's work and any measures not included in the plan. It should clearly show for each section and each individual, how far the set tasks have been carried out, what results have been attained and in what direction it is proposed to pursue the work.

Reference must be made to the numbers of the letters in which the Centre has been informed about the progress of work on specific persons (agent, confidential contacts and prospective cultivations). If there is no information on some section of the report, then this should be stated clearly and directly. Reference should not be made in the report to persons on whom operational information has not been sent to the Centre.

In view of the fact that the report will be sent in by the PR Line, steps should be taken to encode reference to the facilities of other lines which are being used to process American targets, confining mention to the source's (prospect's) pseudonym and line of work.

The following structure is recommended for an operational report:

I. Organization of work

- formulation of the main task carried out by the Residency in its work on the USA during the period under review.
- a list of the principal and intermediate American targets being studied by the Residency, giving the pseudonyms of the officers to whom they are attached.
- existence of a 'main adversary' group or officer responsible for this section and distribution of responsibilities among officers.

II. Study of targets

- the nature of fresh information about targets for penetration in the period under review, and a list of informative and analytical material and consolidated documents about the targets which have been sent to the Centre.
- information about the discovery of target officials and the search for promising persons in relation to the cultivation of targets.

III. Recruitment work

- results of studying and cultivating American citizens (pseudonym of the study target, pseudonym of officer, operational facilities used, discovery of a basis for recruitment, prospects for future work),
- results of study and cultivation of local nationals working in American target installations (on the same pattern);
- results of efforts to acquire and train recruiting agents and ancillary agents with prospects for use against American targets (on the same pattern).

IV Technical operations

- operational yield and information obtained from existing technical operations;

- development of operational and technical prerequisites for carrying out new technical operations, stage of implementation.

V. Infiltration of agents into the USA

- agents, confidential contacts and other operational sources infiltrated into the USA. Information and operational yield from operations carried out.

VI. Information and active measures [influence operations]

- results of the Residency's efforts to obtain political information and carry out active measures in the period under review (statistical data, indicating pseudonyms, sources used and the channels for implementing the active measures).

VII. Conclusions and proposals

- overall assessment of results and the operational significance of these in achieving the main task against the USA.
- reasons for failure to carry out individual points in the plan and steps to rectify the position;
- assessment of the contribution by each officer of the Residency in carrying out assignments against the USA.
- proposals for improving and stepping up work on the USA.

No. 1096/PR/57
06.84

Though the KGB's main targets within the somewhat diffuse American intelligence community were the Central Intelligence Agency (CIA) and the National Security [Sigint] Agency (NSA), its preoccupation during the early 1980s with alleged American plans for a nuclear first strike and the militarization of space led it to take an increasing interest in the Defense Intelligence Agency (DIA) which, it claimed, played 'an active part in working out and preparing the practical steps for delivering a preemptive nuclear strike'. Though much criticized and frequently reorganized since its foundation in 1961, the DIA had an obvious interest for both the KGB and the GRU. It takes part in preparing US National Intelligence Estimates and Special National Intelligence Estimates on, *inter alia*, Soviet strategic forces and terrorism. The DIA also produces the Target Data Inventory (TDI) which serves as a data base for the U.S. National Strategic Target List and the Single Integrated Operational Plan (SIOP).[2]

The Centre's view of the DIA, however, was clouded by conspiracy theory. Its briefing to Residencies interpreted National Security Decision Directive 138 of 2 April 1984, authorizing the DIA to use agents to collect intelligence on terrorism, as a sinister plot 'to use the terrorists in subversive action against the USSR and the countries of the socialist community'.

[ms notes:]
Comr Gornov
Comr Yelin
Comr Brown
Comr Artyom
and all operational personnel of the residency

Lavrov, 11/VII.84
[Nikitenko]

Yuk-1

N 395
Secret
Copy No 1

No. 12156/KR
4.7.84

To Representatives and Residents as listed

DESPATCH OF BRIEFING ON THE DIA AND ITS RESIDENCIES ABROAD

We are sending a briefing on 'Organizing agent penetration operations against the American DIA and its Residencies abroad'.

Our residencies must regard recruitment of DIA officials and agent penetration of elements of the United States military special services as being among their prime tasks aimed at strengthening their position as regards having agents in the American special services in order to obtain in good time secret, including documentary, information in advance about the USA's designs in strategy and military policy, exposing the adversary's plans for preparing to launch a nuclear strike against the USSR.

Please inform your operational staff about this briefing and take additional measures to organize systematic and comprehensive study of DIA targets in your country of residence.

Attachment: Briefing No. 12157/KR, 7 pages, Secret, PN

VADIMOV
[V.V. KIRPICHENKO, First Deputy Head, FCD]
[Ms:]Gordon 17.7

Astakhov
17.7

Attachment to No. 12156/KR　　　　　　　　　　　　　　　Secret.

Copy No 1

'Organizing agent penetration of the United States DIA and its Residencies abroad'

The Defense Intelligence Agency and its apparatus abroad continue to occupy an important position in the American intelligence community.

It is in fact on the DIA and its Residencies operating abroad that the task devolves of obtaining, disseminating and analysing intelligence about military potential, defence measures adopted in other states, and, above all, in the countries of the socialist community. The American military special services play an active part in working out and preparing the practical steps for delivering a preemptive nuclear strike against the principal targets on the territory of the Soviet Union and our allies.

Following the aggressive military policy and strategic plans of the US administration, the DIA prepares directives for the priority tasks of all military intelligence agencies, and consolidated documents for assessing the plans and resources of the likely adversary. It is directly involved in preparing relevant sections of the definitive intelligence material compiled by the apparatus of the Director of Central Intelligence of the USA. A centralized register of all intelligence tasks and the information obtained by the intelligence services of the United States Armed Forces is located at the DIA.

The main operational element of the DIA is the department in charge of the work of military attachés. This element consists of five geographical and five functional departments, each having its own communications centre and administration service and head of department's secretariat. Each of the geographical departments directs the activity of military intelligence Residencies of the countries it covers.

The intelligence services of the United States arms of service occupy an important position among the intelligence agencies of the American military special services: ie the land forces intelligence and security command, the air force intelligence service, the directorate of naval intelligence. Co-ordination of activity and effective control of all these is provided by the DIA.

According to the information which we have, elements of the intelligence services of the various arms are actively engaged in information-gathering through groups and detachments which form part of the different army formations and naval and air force bases of the United States deployed abroad.

As a rule, the DIA legal Residencies function through the military attachés, groups of military advisers and the sections for scientific and technical co-operation in the central military establishments of their countries of residence.

Professional military intelligence officers, officers from technical intelligence sub-units and those from operational tactical intelligence carry out duties as part of their cover function in various military installations of the United States located in third countries (military bases, army HQ, the supreme command apparatus of the arms of services in various parts of the world, communications centres, etc).

In a number of countries where the United States has no official establishments, or where the diplomatic representation does not include military attachés, the DIA posts its representatives as officials of mixed commercial companies, banks, shipping combines, etc.

The number of operational staff at a DIA Residency (excluding the head of the organization and the technical staff) may vary from 1 to 25 or more, depending on the degree of importance attributed to the country of residence in the military plans of the US administration, the agent/operational situation and the prevailing counter-intelligence system in the country.

American military special services personnel are drawn basically from men serving in the various arms of service, including officers, NCOs and ORs. In addition to the military personnel of the DIA, the arms' special services and other special formations engaged in gathering and processing military intelligence, some use is also made of carefully vetted civilians, who, as a rule, form the auxiliary and administrative apparatus of these special services.

Beginning in the 1980s, applications were also invited from final-year students at civilian colleges and universities in the USA. The number of civilian specialists working in the military special services is increasing year by year. A special system of training is organized for this category of personnel, based on the US military intelligence school in Washington, the American Army's institute of foreign languages at Monterey (California) and the US Army intelligence school at Fort Huachuca (Arizona). The largest percentage of graduates from civilian educational establishments employed in the DIA work in the analysis and coding sections, and also in the investigation service and sub-units engaged in scientific and technical intelligence.

Among the general requirements expected of members of the military special services are such qualities as political and moral reliability, an interest in intelligence work, the faculty of understanding and influencing people, and sound physical health.

Members of the DIA are well looked after in the material sense. (Their salaries range from 13 to 30 thousand dollars a year, not counting increments for years of service, rank, etc.) Particular attention is paid to political loyalty. Strict control is exercised over their conduct and way of thinking. In accordance with the instructions from the ministers for the US armed services, from 1982 onwards, all members of military intelligence and counter-intelligence services, who have access to secrets, must sign an undertaking not to divulge secrets. This obligation was in fact in operation during the 1970s, applying even after completion of service in the intelligence or counter-intelligence service. Members of the military special services must report immediately all contacts with foreigners, especially those from socialist countries, to the military counter-intelligence representative and to their immediate superior. The requirement to report to counter-intelligence extends also to contacts of DIA members with other foreigners and even with American citizens whose conduct and actions may prejudice the national security of the USA.

The chief task confronting the DIA and its Residencies consists in obtaining advance information about possible military, economic and political measures adopted in other countries, primarily in the USSR and members of the Warsaw Pact, and also in areas 'vitally important for the national security of the USA'.

As part of the overall intelligence programme and the DIA directive prepared on that basis, the 'list of key issues for military intelligence', the Residencies are called upon to carry out a complete reconnaissance of the most important economic, defence and industrial installations in the territory of the Warsaw Pact member-states which have been marked out as the main targets for a nuclear missile strike.

The following form part of the duties of DIA residencies: to produce timely intelligence data about preparations for an attack on the United States or its allies; about trends and prospects for expansion of the armed forces of countries of the socialist community, and their operational and strategic resources; about plans for operational use of the main groupings of armed forces of the potential adversary, their strength, deployment and armament, counter-intelligence support for the activity of the DIA's stations abroad, in close co-operation with CIA Residencies; and exposure of members of the Soviet IS [intelligence service] and their efforts in regard to the American armed forces; they also carry out penetration operations with agents – in association with the CIA – against Soviet intelligence personnel, using American servicemen to plant on the Soviet intelligence service.

The DIA's instructions in recent years have directed the military intelligence organization abroad to look for indications of increased combat readiness in the groups of Soviet forces deployed in certain East European countries, Afghanistan, and also in Cuban units located in Angola and Ethiopia.

These instructions also apply to the activity of DIA Residencies aimed at clarifying the question of Soviet co-operation with third-world countries. At the same time the organizations abroad are also given, as a long-term assignment, the task of obtaining information about the legal position regarding existing agreements on military matters, any extension of their scope and introduction of new forms of co-operation in that field.

Under Directive No 138 of the President of the United States, which came into operation in April this year, the DIA was invested for the first time with powers to use agents of the military special services for infiltration of terrorist and subversive groups and organizations operating in third countries' territory. At the same time the DIA was officially given the task of expanding the volume of intelligence information obtained on terrorist elements operating immediately around American military formations abroad. The facts, however, indicate that the main, unacknowledged assignment in this context is to use the terrorists in subversive action against the USSR and the countries of the socialist community.

In addition to its intelligence activity abroad, the DIA has counter-intelligence tasks aimed at uncovering Soviet intelligence personnel, hampering their activity and ascertaining the designs of our intelligence service in regard to United States' military installations. This work is carried out in close collaboration with the CIA (in third countries) and the FBI (in the USA).

In their daily activity the Pentagon's central intelligence apparatus and its Residencies are guided by the directive on the 'Tasks of military intelligence and the order of priority in carrying them out'. This document is prepared every year at the DIA headquarters. These tasks are set out in greater detail in the List of key issues for military intelligence which is despatched periodically to all Residencies.

The material available in the Centre provides evidence that the chief sources for obtaining information on the USSR of interest to the DIA and its Residencies are agents, data obtained from space reconnaissance and instrumental means. At the same time the adversary has succeeded in acquiring important information of a strategic nature on aspects in which he is interested by processing overt documentary material and questioning defectors, traitors and immigrants.

Study of the practical methods used in intelligence work by the DIA components based at home and abroad, has shown that American military intelligence makes use for information-gathering purposes of its official and personal contacts with Soviet citizens and in the first place, military attachés and their staff, officers and employees of the Chief Military Advisor's organization, the GIU, GTU and GKES* in third countries.

When present as observers at military exercises held on third countries' territory, DIA officers try to make a wide range of contacts among Soviet military personnel invited on these occassions, put a great many questions to them about the combat characteristics of Soviet-made weapons and military equipment and attempt to obtain basic data on individual Soviet nationals and information on the officers of military units, such as where they are serving and so on.

In the same way, American military intelligence personnel make use

---

* GIU: GRU General Engineering Department (deals with Soviet weapons exports)
GTU: General Technical Department (oversees Soviet military facilities and advisers overseas)
GKES: State Committee for Foreign Economic Relations

of official formal occasions and private receptions organized by them on a great variety of pretexts, *receptions* to which they invite, together with the service diplomats, Soviet Embassy officials, journalists and specialist personnel.

As one method of obtaining intelligence information on Soviet matters, DIA officials and their agents made use of contacts with service diplomats of non-aligned or neutral countries friendly to the USSR, and countries receiving Soviet military equipment, where our military specialists are to be found.

One of the operational methods most frequently used by the American military special services is to attempt to plant on the Soviet intelligence service agents drawn from among American servicemen, making approaches as alleged sympathizers and offering us their services for a material reward. The actual utilization of information obtained by the adversary in the course of such operations is as a rule entrusted to the CIA or the FBI.

The other side naturally devotes a great deal of attention to improving 'plant' operations, trying to avoid stereotyped methods and even going so far as to hand over to us, particularly in the first stages, genuine secret, and sometimes even top secret, information of interest to us.

In view of the role and position of the DIA in the American intelligence community and the amount of important political, strategic and operational information concentrated in United States military intelligence installations, the need to penetrate the adversary's military special services has acquired particular importance for achieving the tasks confronting the intelligence service abroad.

No. 12157/KR

Military Priorities

The Soviet General Staff regards both strategic and tactical military intelligence as the primary responsibility of its Second Chief (Intelligence) Directorate, the GRU (*Glavnoye Razvedyvatelnoye Upravlenie*). The KGB also considered questions of military strategy one of its main global priorities. Because of the partial overlap in their operations, relations between the KGB and the GRU have from time to time been fraught both in Moscow and in foreign Residencies.[3] The KGB, however, was larger, better funded and able to pull rank on what it called its 'military neighbours'. Though the GRU's interests are usually defended by the Minister of Defence, none of its heads has ever been even a candidate (non-voting) member of the Politburo. By contrast, Yuri Vladimirovich Andropov, KGB Chairman from 1967 to 1982, became Party General Secretary from 1982 to 1984.[4] Viktor Mikhailovich Chebrikov, Chairman from 1982 to 1988, became a full member of the Politburo in 1985 at a time when the Minister of Defence was only a candidate member. Kryuchkov, his successor as KGB Chairman, also became a full Politburo member in 1989. (Though he left the Politburo after its reorganization and downgrading in 1990, he became a member of Gorbachev's short-lived Presidential Council; early in 1991 he joined the newly created National Security Council.)

The KGB's main military concern during the early 1980s was the threat of a nuclear first strike by the West: a fear which produced its largest ever peacetime intelligence operation and its first major collaboration with the GRU, Operation RYAN. But it was also haunted by the strategic nightmare of the Soviet Union's four main adversaries – the USA, Western Europe, Japan and China – coming together to form 'a large-scale anti-Soviet (anti-Communist) military coalition'.

[ms notes:]
  Comr Gornov, Shatov,
    Brown, Artyom and
    all operational staff of the
    Residency for guidance in
    our work
        LAVROV [L.Y. NIKITENKO] 26.12.84

vn-1   Top Secret
No. 2106/PR   Copy No 1
17.12.84   To Residents

MEASURES DESIGNED TO STEP UP WORK ON PROBLEMS OF MILITARY
STRATEGY

The dangerous development in the world situation at the present time
requires our Service to take additional measures to step up its work on
questions of military strategy to the maximum extent in all lines of
activity in the interests of providing reliable protection for state
security and strengthening our country's defence capability.

In this context, under Instruction No 8ss of 10.11.84 from the heads
of our Service, a list of priority strategic questions for the information
of our officers abroad has now come into effect, and requirements have
been formulated for stepping up efforts designed to discover in good
time the aims, scale and time limits envisaged in our main adversary's
preparation for war. The principal objective of this activity continues
to be timely discovery of any intentions of the USA, NATO or the PRC
to carry out a sudden nuclear missile attack on the Soviet Union and
other countries of the socialist community.

In planning and implementing the actual measures intended to deal
with this problem, residencies will concentrate their efforts on the
following:

– obtaining reliable and, first of all, documentary information about
   preparations by our main adversary to take political decisions and
   adopt specific operational plans and measures directed to launching a nuclear or conventional war against the Soviet Union and the
   other countries of the socialist community, or to intensifying

existing, or creating new critical situations which might lead to war;

- acquiring reliable data about any breakthrough achieved by the main adversary in the scientific and technical fields which would enable them to produce radically new types and systems of weapons of mass destruction calculated to shift the strategic balance of forces sharply in their favour;
- preparing and implementing large-scale active measures to expose enemy plans and designs for preparing for war.

In planning and pursuing work on the problems of military strategy you must be strictly guided by the attached list of priority strategic questions.

Attachment: As indicated in text, top secret, 10 pages. No 8ss

SVETLOV

[N.P. GRIBIN]

[Head of Third Department, FCD]

Attachment to No 2106/PR

LIST OF PRIORITY QUESTIONS OF MILITARY STRATEGY ON WHICH THE INTELLIGENCE SERVICE ABROAD IS REQUIRED TO THROW LIGHT

I. Strategic, economic and military fields

1.1 New features in both coalition and national military policy doctrines, military strategy and the strategic designs of the political and military leadership of the United States, the NATO bloc, the principal West European countries and Japan, and also the PRC, envisaging stepping up long-term and immediate preparation for and possible launching of a nuclear or conventional war against the USSR and other countries of the socialist community:

- views entertained by the leadership on the possible scale and nature,

targets and missions, and ways and means of preparation, launching and conduct of a war;
- place, role and specific plans for preparing and carrying out a sudden nuclear missile strike.

1.2 Estimates by senior political and military figures in the USA, the NATO bloc, the main West European countries and Japan, and the PRC analysing and forecasting any important changes in the world military, political and strategic situation:

- in the overall correlation of military forces between West and East;
- in the correlation of military forces in areas bordering on the USSR;
- in the correlation of military forces in areas distant from the USSR;

1.3 International political, economic and other circumstances and situations in which the USA, the NATO bloc, the principal West European countries and Japan, and also the PRC may reach the stage of launching a nuclear or conventional war:

- large-scale social, political and economic shifts anticipated in individual areas or countries which may transgress the limits (thresholds) they have set for qualitative changes in the military and strategic situation;

1.4 Military policy decisions, designs, plans and measures of the United States, NATO, principal West European and Japanese military policy leaders to bring together a large-scale anti-Soviet (anti-communist) military coalition, or to strengthen existing and create new military blocs and associations of imperialist states:

- expansion and intensification of military consultations as part of multilateral conferences and summit meetings, bilateral talks and agreements on mutual security and defence, strategic partnering and co-operation;
- attempts to create a 'global security system' involving the United States, Western Europe and Japan;
- expansion of the membership and areas of responsibility of NATO, the Western European Union (WEU), the Organization of American States (OAS), the regional security and defence system in the Caribbean;

- attempts to form a European Union (EU), a Pacific Treaty Organization (PATO), a North-East Asia Treaty Organization (NEATO), a Middle East Treaty Organization (METO), or a South Atlantic Treaty Organization (SATO).

1.5 Present position and prospects for a military policy and strategic rapprochement between the USA, the NATO bloc, the principal West European countries and Japan, and the PRC, on an anti-Soviet basis:

- specific designs, plans and measures of the military and political leadership of the USA and its allies aimed at drawing China into military, political and economic relations with the West;
- the contents of existing and possible new military agreements between the USA and its allies and the PRC (assistance to China in developing defence industry and nuclear power, and in acquiring modern types of armaments and military equipment, and the technology for producing them);
- strategic provocation and incitement on the part of the PRC leadership.

1.6 Directives, combined programmes, plans and measures to augment the military and economic potential of the USA, the NATO bloc, the main West European countries and Japan, and also the PRC for the purpose of long-term and immediate preparation for the possibility of launching and waging a nuclear or conventional war;

- drawing up and implementing coalition and national policies for appropriations and expenditure for military requirements, and distribution of combined efforts to produce the basic types of weapon and military equipment;
- providing for maximum capacity in production facilities of military branches of industry and creating fresh capacity, and switching a number of civilian branches to production on military lines;
- creating large-scale strategic reserves of military industrial equipment, energy resources and raw materials in short supply, foodstuffs, military stores and medical supplies;
- expanding trade in armaments, granting loans and credits and offering military economic, scientific and technical aid.

1.7 Any directives or instructions, drafts, plans or measures on the part of those directing military policy in the USA, the NATO bloc, the principal West European countries and Japan, and also the PRC to upgrade the structure of the main branches of the armed forces, or provide them with up-to-date types of weapons and equipment;

- reinforcing the organization and stepping up the numerical strength and quality of the establishment of strategic nuclear and other armed forces (ground-based intercontinental ballistic missiles, warships and submarines, strategic bomber and fighter air forces, artillery and armour);
- reinforcing the presence of strategic armed forces on advanced ocean and maritime positions in the most important areas and countries (deployment close to the Soviet Union of American naval and air forces, extended and medium-range nuclear missiles, cruise missiles and other weapons, advance stock-piling of nuclear ammunition and munitions, and preparation and modernization of naval and air bases required for this purpose);
- improving the strategic mobility of the main branches of the armed forces (expansion of facilities for rapid movement of large airborne formations and units, ammunition and logistical and technical supplies, using ocean-going and sea-going shipping and military transport aircraft);
- stepping up the permanent operational readiness of the basic complement of intercontinental ballistic missiles, extended and medium-range ballistic missiles, warships and submarines, strategic air force and early warning posts;
- organizing and carrying out strategic command-post, naval, air, army and specialist exercises with senior coalition and national political and military command echelons, staff and command posts taking part in preparing different variants of mobilization deployment of reserve components, operational deployment of the armed forces and various arms, testing their battle readiness and capability for delivery of nuclear and other strikes in possible theatres of war and military action;
- organizing and improving the work of central and local agencies for providing for the survival of the administrative apparatus, the economy and the civilian population in conditions of nuclear or conventional war;

1.8 Directives, projects, plans and measures on the part of the USA, NATO, the main West European countries and Japan and also the PRC, associated with a possible switch to immediate preparation for launching and conducting a nuclear or conventional war;

- preparation, adoption and implementation of major political and military decisions for eventually launching and waging a war; (selection of specific ways, places and dates for going into action, modification of combined and specialized operational plans for the conduct of the war);
- bringing the higher administrative and military command, control and communications systems into a state of full combat readiness (transferring the administrative and military leadership to wartime command posts, and putting new control and communication facilities into operation);
- gradual or urgent switching of strategic nuclear and conventional armed forces to a state of full combat readiness, according to the prescribed alert system;
- immediate preparation for carrying out a sudden nuclear attack (definition of the main sectors and objectives of nuclear and other operations in the initial period of the war).

1.9 Military strategy directives and aims, designs, plans and measures, and political and military decisions of the military and political leadership of the United States, the NATO bloc, the principal West European countries, Japan, and also the PRC, relating to preparing, launching and conducting limited regional and local wars and stirring up existing and creating fresh foci of international tension, military conflicts and crisis situations;

- attempts to regain positions lost in the developing countries and destabilize and change existing regimes;
- improvement of combat capabilities and operational utilization of the national armed forces of developing countries where pro-American or pro-Chinese forces are in power;
- creating, deploying and stepping up the combat capabilities of rapid-deployment and special-purpose forces on foreign territory;
- independent, combined or co-ordinated acts of direct and indirect

aggression (armed intervention in the internal affairs of other countries and organizing and infiltrating guerrilla formations).

1.10 Opposition of the political and military leadership of the United States, the NATO bloc, the main West European countries and Japan, and also the PRC to the peace initiatives of the USSR and the other countries of the socialist community;

- on the questions of preserving and promoting peace, ensuring international security, political and military détente, full or partial disarmament, and reducing and eliminating the threat of war;
- on regional problems of preserving peace and security, settling existing and preventing fresh armed conflicts and crisis situations;
- on questions of normalizing bilateral relations.

II. Science, engineering and technology

2.1 Directives from the military policy leaders, programmes, plans and activity of military, industrial and scientific research institutions in the USA, the NATO bloc, the main countries of Western Europe, and Japan, and also the PRC designed to increase military technology potential, with a view to long-term and immediate preparation, launching and conduct of a nuclear or conventional war.

- stepping up fundamental, pure and applied scientific research and development which might lead to considerable improvement in existing types or to creating radically new types of strategic and tactical nuclear and conventional weapons;
- active utilization of important inventions and discoveries, and designs and ideas for military technology, which would ensure that a really new qualitative level was reached in the upgrading of individual types of strategic and tactical nuclear and conventional weapons.

2.2 Scientific, design and construction and technological documentation and samples from industrial firms, and scientific centres, revealing results and prospects for utilizing research and development, their tactical and technical characteristics, design features, production technology and testing of existing nuclear weapons, and those in process of development and also non-nuclear systems designed for dealing with strategic problems;

- land-based and naval strategic missile systems (MX, Midgetman, 'Trident-2', future developments);
- strategic and tactical aircraft capable of carrying nuclear weapons ('B-1' bombers, ATV ('Stealth'), B-52H modifications, F-14, F-18, Super-Mirage 4000, F-25 fighters, and future developments);
- strategic and operational tactical, land, sea or air-based cruise missiles and remote-piloted aircraft;
- nuclear munitions;
- anti-submarine defence facilities, including acoustic protection for submarines, sonar search equipment and non-acoustic submarine detection facilities;
- anti-missile and anti-aircraft defence systems with ground-, air-, and space-based elements (present position, prospects for development and utilization);
- control, communications and counter-intelligence systems (C^3I) of the armed forces;
- chemical and biological weapons and protection devices against weapons of mass destruction;
- special high-power laser-based weaponry for anti-missile and anti-space systems, naval and air force equipment and also pencil-beam and rapid-fire weapons;
- reusable space transport systems and long-term orbital stations used for military purposes;
- electronic warfare systems and weapons and also ECM [electronic counter-measures] for enemy detection and control systems;
- high-energy fuels and explosives;
- geophysical weapons (deliberate effects produced on weather and climate and the ionosphere, and triggering off earthquakes and tsunamis);
- non-nuclear weapons systems designed for strategic purposes (means of delivery and tactical control, systems for homing on a target enhanced effect warhead charges);
- programmes for introducing new technology and production methods for military equipment;
- present position and prospects for developing the main components

of the PRC's nuclear potential; the PRC's nuclear, space-missile, aviation and electronics industries.

III. Military strategy aspects of the intelligence and counter-intelligence activities of the special services

3.1 Directives, orders and tasks of the military policy leadership of the USA, the NATO bloc, the principal West European countries and Japan, and also the PRC for providing intelligence and counter-intelligence support for implementing military strategy and operational/tactical measures:

- extent of information of the military policy leaders regarding major changes in the military and strategic situation in the world, in the most important regions and countries, and about military policy decisions, plans and measures, economic and technical military potential, the armed forces and armament of the USSR and the Warsaw Pact Organization and individual socialist countries, and their readiness and capabilities regarding reciprocal retaliatory strategic operations in eventual theatres of war and military action;
- the considerable increase in the activity of the adversary's military strategic and operational/tactical intelligence service using agent and technical penetration against important political, military and economic targets in the USSR and the other countries of the socialist community, in order to obtain reliable strategic information and undermine military and economic potential and morale (reinforcing existing sub-sections of strategic intelligence and creating new ones for this purpose, improving their organization and establishment, facilities and resources, and methods of operation);
- specific plans and measures to acquire and infiltrate agents in the territory of the USSR and that of countries of the socialist community, reactivating operations with agents put 'on ice', creating a reserve agent apparatus, making arrangements for maintaining reliable communications with them, and providing the necessary electronic and technical equipment for this purpose;
- expansion and active exploitation by hostile intelligence services of space, air, sea and land observation posts for picking up and intercepting information;
- reinforcement of existing large-scale diversionary reconnaissance

and sabotage formations, detachments and groups, and creation of new ones for eventual action in the rear of the armed forces of the USSR and its allies;

– imposing a stricter counter-intelligence system in the adversary's higher political and military institutions, armed forces and arms of service, headquarters and command posts, the military branches of industry, large corporations and firms, and scientific research centres;

– material prepared and submitted by the adversary's intelligence and counter-intelligence services, including analytical and forecasting assessments, proposals and recommendations on strategic questions, providing assistance for working out, adopting and implementing political and military decisions, designs and plans involved in long-term and immediate preparation for, and eventual launching and conduct of, a nuclear or conventional war.

No 8 ss

Residency Priorities: The Case of Denmark

Residencies around the world had two distinct responsibilities: first, operations against American, NATO and Chinese targets; secondly, operations against the host country. The Copenhagen Residency, where Gordievsky was stationed as a Line N (illegal support) officer from 1966 to 1970 and as a Line PR (political intelligence) officer from 1973 to 1978, was a fairly typical case in point. The three-year operational 'plan of work' drawn up in 1976 by the Resident, Mikhail Petrovich Lyubimov, for the penetration of the Danish Foreign Ministry and Prime Minister's Office, was intended to acquire intelligence on American and NATO, as well as Danish, policy:

No 687/PR   Top Secret
13 October 1976   Copy No.1
From Copenhagen   To Moscow

PLAN OF WORK AGAINST THE PRIME MINISTER'S OFFICE AND THE
DANISH MINISTRY OF FOREIGN AFFAIRS (OVER A 3-YEAR PERIOD)

The Office of the Prime Minister and the Ministry of Foreign Affairs (MFA) are important targets in Denmark, the penetration of which represents a permanent requirement for the work of the Residency.

The Prime Minister's Office is formally considered to be one of the Danish ministries. It is located in the same building as the MFA (the Christiansborg Castle); the majority of offices of both departments are on one and the same floor of this building. The staff of the Prime Minister's Office consists of 40 officials and roughly the same number of technical assistants.

The hub of the Prime Minister's Office is the Secretariat through which passes all kinds of information relating to external and internal political affairs. Part of this information on external affairs is unique in its way, as it reaches the office, bypassing the MFA, by virtue of direct exchanges between the Heads of Government of the Western countries.

The Danish MFA has at its disposal a variety of external political information which is of essential interest to our Service, in particular that which relates to such questions as NATO, the relations between East and West, the relations with the USA, political co-operation within the EEC, the fulfilment of the CSCE [Conference on Security and Co-operation in Europe] resolutions. Communications and reports are received here from Danish Embassies abroad, and there is information which comes by way of exchanges between the countries of NATO, the EEC and Northern Europe.

In organizing a deep study of the Danish MFA with the object of devoting the Residency's efforts to the most important areas, we have singled out those units of the Ministry where information of the greatest interest to us is concentrated:

a) the Political Department of the MFA (which consists of three sections);
b) the third section of the Administrative Department which is responsible for questions of security, for communications and cipher traffic;
c) the Political Economic Department;
d) the second section of the commercial department which is responsible for economic relations with the Socialist countries and also responsible for the control over the export of strategic goods.

We are planning the following steps in our intensive study of the Prime Minister's Office and the Danish MFA:

1. To use the Residency's confidential contacts and operational contacts ...* for gathering information about the activity of the Prime Minister's Office and about the MFA; also to obtain leads to officials within these establishments; ...*
2. Fundamental attention in our efforts to study these targets will be assigned to acquiring agent recruiters. This task will be executed within the framework of the Residency's overall work plan against the Main Adversary [US] target (as set out in our 647/PR of 15 September of this year).
3. We shall collect official information about the activity of both

---

* see explanation on page 28

Ministries, their structure, their regulations concerning recruitmen-tand so on through official contacts among officials of these departments; ...*

4. In carrying out a study of the organization of the technical services of the Prime Minister's Office and the MFA we shall pay particular attention to the third section of the Administrative Department which handles all kinds of communications including courier service, the cipher services, protection, etc. We shall make efforts to home in on cipher officials of the Danish MFA. A report will be submitted about the activities of this section; ...*

5. Measures will be taken to acquire information about the training and recruitment of officials of the most important elements of the technical services of the MFA: cipher clerks, couriers, employees in the photographic laboratories and printing sections, radio operators, telephonists and others. We shall seek to clarify whether a special school or courses exist for training cipher clerks for the MFA and other Danish government institutions. A report will be prepared on the above-mentioned questions;

6. We shall delve into the working conditions of the technical secretaries of the directing staff of the Prime Minister's Office and the MFA and establish to what extent they have access to secret documents;

   We shall identify the training places and recruitment programmes for secretaries, typists, stenographers and female assistants in the offices and for the archive assistants;

   We shall prepare a report on these questions; ...*

7. We shall make a detailed study of the way in which the operational staff acquire their jobs in the MFA. We shall clarify from which training institutions (including from which faculties and from which department within the various faculties) new officials are recruited, how the transfer of staff between various government departments is carried out. We shall take steps to get information about the methods and depths of the checks which the personnel section of the Administrative Department of the MFA carries out on new entrants; ...*

8. After preliminary study we shall try to select from among the technical personnel of the MFA a candidate for deep cultivation and subsequent recruitment through Line N [illegal-support] assets. We shall prepare an appropriate proposal; ...*

---

* see explanation on page 28.

9. We shall study the possibilities of carrying out a technical opera-
tion† in the MFA buildings or in the flats of its officials. We shall
consider the exploitation of possibilities by Line OT [operational-
technical] in connection with the construction which has already
begun of a new building for the Danish MFA at Christianshavn (an
area of Copenhagen). ...*

KORIN
[M P LYUBIMOV]
[Resident in Copenhagen]

* Pseudonyms of contacts and Residency officers, and target dates for submission of progress reports, omitted.
† the planting of bugging devices

During the later 1970s the Copenhagen Residency claimed to
be able to influence the Danish peace movement in anti-
American and pro-Soviet directions, as well as to launch
counter-attacks against American complaints at the abuse of
human rights in the Soviet Union. In 1977 FCD Service A, which
was responsible for 'active measures' (influence operations),
composed a number of letters which it wished to be sent to
Rosalynn Carter, wife of the US President, protesting against
American 'infringement of human rights'. The Copenhagen
Residency persuaded a well-known liberal politician to despatch
one of these letters to Mrs Carter, and sent a triumphant
telegram to the Centre announcing its success.

As usual, KGB active measures in Denmark were co-ordinated
with overt and semi-covert influence operations orchestrated by
the International Department. In October 1977 the International
Department took the initiative in arranging a hearing in Copenhagen sponsored by the main Soviet front organization, the
World Peace Concil, to denounce the West German *Berufsver-
bot*: a ban on various categories of left-wingers occupying
certain jobs. The Copenhagen Residency, meanwhile, was
covertly promoting allegations that 'militaristic and neo-fascist
forces were coming to the fore' in the Federal Republic.[5]

The Residency's PR Line (political intelligence) Work Plan for
1978 set out a highly ambitious programme both of intelligence
collection and of active measures:

No 907/PR   Top Secret
8 December 1977   Copy No 1
Copenhagen   To Moscow
                    To: Comrade Severov [Grushko]

THE COPENHAGEN RESIDENCY'S PR LINE WORK PLAN FOR 1978

The Residency sees the following requirements as its basic objectives
for 1978:

- the penetration of Main Adversary targets, in the first instance by
  the acquisition of support agents from among the local population;
- similarly to aim for agent penetration of the main local institutions
  of intelligence interest to us: the Danish MFA and the Prime
  Minister's Office;
- to carry on Line K work [against China] on the basis that agent
  penetration of the Chinese People's Republic embassy in Denmark
  is the most important requirement; and to continue the deep study
  of the British and FRG embassies;
- to proceed with the systematic collection of current political intelligence, relating in the first place to the most important questions:
  the policies of the USA, NATO and the EEC, and also questions
  which directly affect the interests of the Soviet Union;
- to mount active political measures designed to support USSR
  foreign policy, with particular regard to their complexity and
  international character.

In carrying out its intelligence work the Residency will be guided by
instructions from the leadership of the [Third] Department* and
Service [FCD] and, in particular, by the recommendations and comments expressed in your letter No 2097/PR of 3.11.1977.

1. The Residency's PR Line requirements

a. Intelligence-gathering work

The primary efforts of the Residency's case officers during 1978 will be

---

* The FCD Third Department was responsible for KGB operations in Britain, Ireland,
Scandinavia, Australasia and Malta.

directed towards obtaining intelligence on the military-political and subversive plans of the USA, NATO and China towards the USSR and other countries of the socialist community, on United States policy towards Western Europe and the situation on the northern flank of the North Atlantic bloc. Residency officers will also be endeavouring to obtain intelligence on the place and role of Denmark in NATO, on new developments and trends in the policies of Denmark towards the Soviet Union and the other socialist countries, on the plans for the gradual transformation of the EEC into a military-political union and on Danish policies within the framework of the Nine and Northern Europe.

The Residency is planning to submit to the Centre on a regular basis analyses on the political situation in the country and on the plans of the Social Democrats to improve their position, the state of affairs in the bourgeois parties, subversive activity on the part of the rightist forces against the Communist Party and against links between the USSR and Denmark.

Coverage and interpretation of important international conferences, meetings and negotiations will continue, whether these are held in Denmark or in other West European countries, including the final stage of the Belgrade Conference, the meeting of Heads of State and governments of the Nine in Copenhagen in April 1978, etc ...

b. Line A Work [Active Measures]

The main thrust of our active measures work will be as follows:

i. The exertion of influence on Danish political and social circles with relation to the questions of détente, East – West relations, the fulfilment of CSCE [Conference on Security and Co-operation in Europe] decisions and the decisions of the Belgrade Conference in a way which benefits Soviet policies. The harnessing of support for Soviet peace proposals, for the policy of disarmament, for the conduct of the campaign against the Neutron bomb, Cruise missiles and other new types of weaponry, in whose production the USA has a stake. ...

An important role will be played in this work by the Jutland Committee for Peace and Security, which was formed with our participation and also by the All Danish Co-ordinating Committee for Peace, Security and Co-operation, in the leadership of which our contacts are active. ...

ii. The countering of US and NATO activity designed to increase Denmark's dependence on the bloc; the exposure of US policies which aim to heighten the degree of dependence of the Western European countries.

The exposure of violation of human rights in the USA. The publication of X's* book-album in the FRG and Sweden and helping to secure its appearance in Britain. Assisting the activities of X's* exhibition-show. The study of the feasibility of putting on the exhibition in other Western countries.

The disclosure of the increase in the activities of militaristic and neo-fascist forces in the FRG and the efforts of that country to play a dominant role in the EEC. The exposure of the attempts of the ruling circles in countries of Western Europe to transform the EEC into a military-political union.

In order to perform these tasks we intend to make use of speeches and broadcasts, based on our theses, by our agents and contacts in Parliament, in the press and on television and to complete the publication and distribution of a pamphlet which condemns the opponents of détente. ...

We aim to increase the efficiency of the channel through which influence may be exerted on the Prime Minister. ...

iii. The broadening of ways of bringing influence to bear on public opinion in the Western countries to our advantage. Efforts also to make use of effective mass information media such as television, the cinema and radio. With this in mind we must ensure the successful implementation through 'X'* of the [anti-US] operation and the actions associated with it. We must also ensure that this operation influences other countries of Northern Europe, in particular Sweden and Norway. ...

iv. The discrediting of the policies of the Chinese People's Republic, which are aimed at supporting NATO and the EEC against the Soviet Union, and at undermining the international and communist movement.

Attention will be given, in 1978, to perfecting the various forms of active measures, endowing them with a complex character, with the aim of transcending national frameworks, and also so that new operational possibilities can be provided and instigated.

---

* an agent recruited by the Line PR officer, Nikolai Petrovich Gribin, later Resident in Copenhagen from 1980 to 1984.

2. Operational Measures designed to fulfil the Residency's Requirements

a) Basic targets for agent penetration Main Adversary work

The Main Adversary work will be conducted in accordance with the Centre's instructions and the Residency's three-year forward plan (No 647/PR of 15.9.76). We propose to concentrate on the acquisition of support agents (mainly agent-recruiters and talent-spotters) able to fulfil our requirements, of which the most important is agent penetration of American targets.

Specifically, the planning for 1978 includes the following:

- to continue the study of Main Adversary targets, paying special attention to the US Embassy as the prime target of interest to us. In order to collect interesting information on it we shall continue the practice of meetings with specifial American diplomats. In order to widen contacts among embassy officials it is proposed to hold a variety of meetings on an official basis (film shows, sporting competitions, evening events etc). ...
- to carry out a purposeful search for individuals among the technical staff of the US Embassy and other Main Adversary targets to select subjects for deep study. To endeavour to create conditions for making use of Line N [illegal support] facilities in this work.
- to continue observation of the living quarters of the technical staff. Cafés, bars and discothèques where Americans in this category spend their leisure time will be regularly visited. We shall try to identify living quarters of the technical staff and their places of leisure not previously known to the Residency. ...
- to step up the study of X*'s contacts, directing him to persons of immediate interest from the point of view of work against the Main Adversary and bearing in mind their possible future recruitment under a 'false flag' by X*. ...
- to complete the recruitment of ... to utilize him as agent-recruiter and talent spotter for Main Adversary work;
- through operational contacts available to the Residency and using other facilities, to search for a candidate for the role of penetration agent into one of the Main Adversary targets (or an appropriate department of the Danish MFA) in the capacity of a technical employee. We shall increase the practice of utilizing case officers' wives for this task. ...

---

* see footnote on page 31

– to continue the study of Americans (permanently or temporarily resident in Denmark) from the ranks of businessmen, journalists, teachers, students etc, …

Prime Minister's Office (Pseudonym 'TEREM' – Dungeon)

In the work of studying this target for penetration by us in 1978, special attention must be paid to the identification from among 'TEREM' staff (especially from among the female technical staff) of those with whom we may try to establish contact, with a view to their future deep study. With the same object in view we shall also identify the procedures for training and recruiting secretaries, shorthand typists and other female staff of the 'TEREM'. In our study of 'TEREM', use will be made of information obtained from people working there … and various official material. …

The Danish Ministry of Foreign Affairs (Pseudonym 'SOBOR' – Cathedral)

Considering that Residency officer have a significant number of official contacts with this target it is proposed to concentrate our main efforts in 1978 on a study of that part which presents the greatest interest from the point of view of penetration and the acquisition of valuable operational intelligence, namely the third office of the administrative department which incorporates all aspects of communications including couriers, the cipher service and also security protection etc. Work will be initiated to obtain intelligence on the most important sub-units of the 'SOBOR' technical services, the identity of couriers, photography laboratory workers, secretaries and shorthand typists, together with their access to secret documents. …
(The study of the 'SOBOR' [MFA] and the 'TEREM' [Prime Minister's Office] as a whole will be effected with due regard to the three-year plan, No 687/PR of 1976).

Institutions linked to the EEC

The work on the penetration of basic EEC targets in Denmark will be continued in 1978 in accordance with our forward plan (No 677/PR of 30.9.76). Fundamental attention in this undertaking will be paid to the Danish MFA where basic documents relating to the Ministry of Commerce, the Information Offices of the EEC Commission and the

European Parliament are concentrated. In connection with Denmark's Chairmanship of the Nine which takes effect from 1 January 1978 we plan a further increase of our work on the EEC. ...

The KGB had a vested interest in exaggerating the impact of its active measures. In Copenhagen, as in a number of other capitals, the Residency sought to claim the credit for a whole series of anti-war and anti-American activities which, in reality, it had done little to promote. Gordievsky believes that active measures during his years in Denmark had only a marginal impact. The Centre, however, considered that 'a significant number' were so strikingly successful that it reported them to the Politburo. During 1977 it 'singled out for special mention' 'a complex of operations' involving a book of unflattering photographs of life in the United States.

No 3208/PR/55   Top Secret
16 January 1977 (*sic*, for 1978)   Copy No 1
    To Copenhagen: Comrade KORIN [LYUBIMOV]

We are sending you herewith an evaluation of the Residency's Active Measures work in 1977 prepared by the appropriate sub-section of our service:

A significant volume of work in the Active Measures field was carried out by the Residency during 1977. Forty-five requirements were placed on the Residency of which 15 were not fulfilled (these were basically of a non-European nature) and a number of operations were implemented through the Residency's own initiative. Among the operations carried out were:

21 conversations of influence
 9 speeches in Parliament
20 public speeches
10 speeches on radio and television
46 publications
 4 documentary operations*
 2 books published

---

* articles and forgeries produced by Service A.

6 meetings and demonstrations
2 exhibitions
7 items of material distributed and a number of other measures

A significant number of active measures implemented through the Residency's own resources received favourable appraisal and were the subjects of reports to the leadership of our department, of our service and to higher authority.* The complex of operations involving the publishing, distribution and publicizing of the book 'American Pictures' should be singled out for special mention.

Active measures work was correctly organized by the Residency and its resources were rightly channelled towards aiding the resolution of the top priority foreign policy tasks facing the Soviet Union, such as détente and the Belgrade Conference, disarmament, exposure of the mendacious character of the human rights campaign unleashed by the USA, the exposure of US and NATO plans to develop and deploy new types of weapons etc. Some successful operations were also put into effect against the adversary's subversive ideological centres and against Western special services.

As a rule the Residency effectively carries out the requirements received from the Centre, reports competently and fully on the work done and shows initiative.

Side by side with the positive results which have been mentioned, there have been some shortcomings in the Residency's performance, the elimination of which would contribute to further perfecting its techniques in the active measures field. In particular, cases were noted of requirements not being spelled out clearly enough to sources; also there were cases where a check on their performance was inadequate, with the result that there was some slippage in the political texture of the operations. Often one was aware of the lack of sound channels for carrying out incisive operations against the northern flank of NATO and the USA, for stepping up anti-NATO and anti-American feeling in Denmark, for urging the Social-Democratic government to cut down on the country's participation in the military preparations of the [NATO] bloc, and for exposure of the activities of Western special services, etc.

A number of measures were carried out by the Residency which were designed to exert influence on the higher echelons of the Danish

---

* *Instantsiya* in Russian. In KGB documents, denotes the highest political leadership, specifically the Party Politburo

government concerning the most important international problems and, judging from available information, successful results were achieved in some cases. In our opinion these possibilities may also be utilized in the future but the work must be undertaken in a more purposeful manner, without losing the initiative. It is evident that the Residency itself should do more to promote the discussion of topics favourable to us, but with the Residency taking the lead and not the target, as has sometimes been the case.

SEVEROV

[GRUSHKO]

[Head of Third Department, FCD]

The Federal Republic of Germany (FRG)

After the 'Main Adversary', the Centre's chief targets were the United States' NATO allies. When NATO was founded in 1949, KGB operations in Britain were still achieving some spectacular successes. Kim Philby was about to be posted to Washington as SIS head of station and liaison officer with the Americans. Donald Maclean and Guy Burgess were supplying large amounts of high-grade intelligence from the Foreign Office and diplomatic service. By the 1970s, however, the golden age of the London Residency was past. After the mass expulsion of 105 KGB and GRU officers from London in 1971, the KGB found operations in Britain more difficult to conduct than in almost any other major Western State.

The Federal Republic of Germany had replaced Britain as the most vulnerable of the major NATO members. The post-war division of Germany and the flow of refugees from the East had made the Federal Republic, which joined NATO in 1955, an easier target for Soviet bloc intelligence penetration than any other West European state. The KGB base at Karlshorst in the Berlin suburbs was the biggest outside the Soviet Union. The foreign intelligence agency of the East German Ministry of State Security, the HVA, was even more successful than the KGB. Its head for 33 years, General 'Mischa' Wolf, had a reputation as the ablest, as well as the longest-serving, of the Soviet bloc intelligence chiefs. Among the most remarkable of his several thousand agents in the Federal Republic was Gunther Guillaume, who for five years was the trusted secretary and personal companion of the West German Chancellor, Willy Brandt. The shock caused by Guillaume's arrest in 1974 led to Brandt's resignation.[6] From time to time the East German leader Erich Honecker boasted openly about the HVA's successes. He said on television in 1976:

We do not intend to publish the reports of our secret service about the situation in the Federal Republic, the Bonn government, the leadership of the CDU/CSU [the Christian Democrats and their Bavarian allies], or the Federal Defence Ministry. There can be no doubt, however, that we are quite well informed. On that subject we rightly feel optimistic.[7]

As well as being kept informed by Mischa Wolf of most high-grade HVA intelligence from the FRG, the KGB had a smaller but important West German network of its own. In 1972 the Soviet diplomat, Arkadi Nikolayevich Shevchenko (later to defect), was shown a number of classified telegrams from the KGB Resident in Bonn, Ivan Ivanovich Zaitsev, which he found 'surprising in the quality and quantity of their information'. He asked the Foreign Ministry's German expert, Valentin Mikhailovich Falin (later head of the International Department), 'how we could obtain such inside intelligence'. Falin 'smiled mysteriously and would say only, "We have quite a net in West Germany, you know" '. Vladimir Mikhailovich Kazakov, then head of the FCD American desk (later Main Resident in Washington from 1979 to 1985), called the FRG 'our door to the West'.[8]

The Centre, however, was worried by the media exposure which followed the arrest of Guillaume and other Soviet bloc spies. 'The campaign of spy-mania and anti-Sovietism', it complained, had made its work in West Germany 'considerably more difficult'. In 1977 Kryuchkov issued a directive informing Residents that 'a pressing need has arisen to expand the spread of intelligence work against the FRG, stepping up the cultivation and study of West Germans in third countries for this purpose'.

gn 1   TOP SECRET
2412/PR/60   Copy No 1
26 July 1977   To Residents (according to the list)

Work against West Germany is assuming an increasingly greater importance at the present time in connection with the growth of the economic potential of the FRG and the increase in its influence in the solution of important international issues.

The Federal Republic of Germany is both economically and militarily the leading West European capitalist country. It is the main strategic bridgehead of NATO, where a significant concentration of the adversary's military strength can be observed: the total numerical strength of the forces of the Western allies (including the Bundeswehr) reaches almost a million in the country. This situation distinguishes the FRG from the other European capitalist states and makes it the most important component of the military bloc. Within the FRG military scientific-research studies in the fields of atomic energy, aviation, rocket construction, electronics, chemistry and biology are being intensively pursued.

Since the FRG has outstripped the other European countries both in industrial production and in its scientific-technical development it has succeeded in filling a leading position within the Common Market and exerting a direct influence on the other members of the Community for the solution of important political questions and for the formulation of a common policy towards the socialist countries.

All this renders it necessary to conduct active intelligence work against West Germany on all lines of intelligence activity.

At the same time the deterioration of agent operational circumstances, the sharp tightening-up of counter-intelligence conditions, the intensive prophylactic operations conducted by the special services against the missions of the socialist countries (and in the first place against the USSR), and continuous fanning of the campaign of spymania and anti-Sovietism have made the activity of our Residencies in the country considerably more difficult.

With a view to overcoming these difficulties and to solving the complex intelligence requirements within compressed time scales, a pressing need has arisen to expand the spread of intelligence work against the FRG, stepping up the cultivation and study of West Germans in third countries for this purpose.

At the present time the FRG has roughly 400 official missions abroad. A large number of West German journalists, advisers and representatives of business circles are to be found in various countries of the world. Over 4 million Germans are living in Western Europe at the present time, while there are roughly 7 million living in the USA and Canada. German colonies in the countries of Latin America, Africa and Asia are expanding as a consequence of the growing penetration of

West German capital into the developing countries. All this creates favourable pre-conditions for the conduct of intelligence work against the FRG within the areas mentioned.

Following on from this particular attention should be paid to planned and well-directed cultivations and studies of West Germans from among the officials of West German missions and international organizations who are in your country of residence, and of officials in local establishments, organizations and firms; and also private persons who have constant contacts with their corresponding counterparts in West Germany. Also worthy of operational attention are colonies of Germans who are permanently resident in the country but who have business, family and other links with the FRG.

An analysis should be prepared of the possibilities open to the Residency, selecting from among the Residency's agent-network suitable candidates from among local citizens who will be capable of fulfilling effectively the role of talent-spotters, cultivators and recruiters, for work against citizens of the FRG and against locally engaged staff of West German institutions; also agents who will be able to go for lengthy stays to the FRG or who can undertake periodic trips to West Germany to collect intelligence of interest to us and to fulfil other operational tasks.

The Annual Reports should contain a reflection of the work which is being carried out against the West Germans.

Keep us informed about all the material which is of operational interest concerning the study and cultivation of West Germans in your country of residence.

ALYOSHIN.
[KRYUCHKOV]

Whatever difficulties the KGB encountered in the FRG were more than compensated over the next decade by the continuing success of Wolf's East German network which maintained a high level of penetration until East Germany itself began to crumble in 1989. Wolf, who had retired two years earlier, took refuge for the next two years in Moscow, where he appears to have assisted the KGB in taking over control of some of his former agents.[9]

Albania

If West Germany was the European state outside the Soviet Bloc on which the KGB was best informed, Albania was probably the European country about which it knew least. In the immediate aftermath of the Second World War and the Communist take-over, according to an Albanian official history, 'The Albanian Communist Party saw in the USSR a sincere, loyal ally and resolute defender of the cause of the Albanian people'. It was believed within the FCD that during the 1950s Soviet leaders had even discussed building holiday villas in Albania. During the Sino-Soviet quarrel, however, Enver Hoxha's neo-Stalinist regime in Tirana sided with Beijing. In 1961 Khrushchev broke off diplomatic relations with Albania, denounced its Party leaders as 'imperialist agents', and urged the Albanian people to overthrow them. Mao, by contrast, declared in 1966: 'Albania is the shining beacon of Socialism in Europe'.

Within Europe, Albania appeared less like a beacon than an international recluse, equally suspicious of contact with both East and West. Hoxha expounded the doctrine of the 'dual adversary', claiming that the Soviet Union and the United States were both superpowers bent on world domination. The beginning of a rapprochement between the United States and China in 1972 thus came as an unpleasant surprise in Tirana. After Mao's death in September 1976, Hoxha eulogized him as 'a great revolutionary' and ordered three days of official mourning. But he remained deeply suspicious of the foreign policy of the new Chinese leadership, warning the Seventh Albanian Party Congress in November 1976: 'You can never lean on one imperialism [the USA] in order to fight the other [the USSR]'.[10]

The first major Centre briefing on Albania after the Seventh Party Congress correctly pointed to signs of a 'a definite cooling in Albanian/Chinese relations'. Remarkably, however, the briefing drew on Western rather than Soviet sources for its analysis.

The breach in diplomatic relations 16 years before had left the
KGB without a legal Residency in Tirana and, apparently, without a significant agent network.

No 969/PR/52   Top Secret
17 February 1977   Copy No 1
              To Residents and Representatives
                    according to a list

THE WEST'S VIEWS ON VARIOUS DEVELOPMENTS IN THE INTERNAL
POLITICAL SITUATION AND FOREIGN POLICY OF ALBANIA AFTER THE
7TH CONGRESS OF THE ALBANIAN LABOUR [COMMUNIST] PARTY

The development of affairs in Albania following the 7th Congress of
the Albanian Labour [Communist] Party (ALP) which took place in
November 1976 continue to attract the attention of Western political
circles. According to assessments by EEC experts the country's
economy is in a 'very serious' state and 'has no prospects of improving'
in the immediate years ahead.

In the same circles it is emphasized that Albania's state economic and
cultural development plan for 1971–75 was revised downwards more
than once, yet all the basic targets remained unfulfilled. The new 5-year
plan approved at the 7th Congress of the ALP envisages a further
slowing down in the tempo of development in the country's national
economy. The intention is over the period 1976–80 to increase industrial output by 41–44 per cent (the 1971–75 plan envisaged 52 per
cent); investment is due to be increased by 33–38 per cent (compared
with the 1971–75 figures of 50 per cent); while turnover is due to
increase by 22–25 per cent (compared with the 1971–75 figures of 50
per cent).

These goals will hardly be achieved in the light of the severe shortage
of raw materials and modern equipment. According to available
information the Albanian government was forced as early as December
1976 to introduce a correction into the five-year plan which had only
just been adopted in order to reduce further a series of objectives.

The decisions taken at the ALP Congress and what has happened on
the basis of these in the succeeding period illustrates that the Albanians
are being guided as before by slogans such as, 'self-help', 'the inten-

sification of the class struggle within the country', and 'the struggle with the imperialist revisionist encirclement'. Among a significant part of the population there continues to be dissatisfaction with their situation and there is hidden displeasure with the political course adopted by the leadership of the ALP. Despite the purges which took place in 1973–76 critical statements about the internal and external policies of the country's leadership are made within a narrow circle by individual members of Albania's party and state apparatus.

As American experts on this subject have commented Hoxha 'realizes the force of the expressions of discontent' in the country and is striving to promote into leading posts people who are devoted to him personally. After the 7th Congress of the ALP Politburo members Isai and Miska, and Mihali, who was a candidate member of the Politburo, became Hoxha's pillars in the Albanian leadership.

In the view of the British Foreign Office new purges amongst the country's leading party and State organs may be expected in the future in Albania. These same conclusions were reached by the leaders of some left-wing groups from West European states who recently visited Albania.

The foreign policy direction of the ALP following the 7th Congress remains anti-Soviet and pro-Chinese. The Albanian leaders assign the basic place in their foreign policy to relations with China. At the same time a definite cooling in Albanian/Chinese relations is observable. In the speeches of the Albanian leaders at the session of the National Assembly in December 1976 China and its new leadership were not mentioned. The Albanian mass information media refrained from giving information about latest events in the PRC. To those leaders who in December 1976 were in Tirana representing a number of the so-called 'Marxist–Leninist' parties, the ALP Central Committee recommended that they should not express a point of view about the events in China until such time as Albania had defined its own position on the matter. The increased friction between Tirana and Peking was also shown by the fact that at the end of December 1976 the two sides were unable to sign a protocol relating to an exchange of goods for 1977.

The main questions that are the cause of discord between Albania and China, in the view of the British Foreign Office, centre on the attitude towards NATO, the 'Common Market' and the non-aligned movement.

The leaders of Albania are not in agreement with the Chinese position on the above-mentioned problems, while the present-day Chinese leadership is unhappy with the external political direction of Albania and with the 'embarrassment' which the Albanians have felt in recent times in connection with the alienation from power of Peking's radicals.

However, neither China nor Albania is interested in a further deepening of discord.

Italian diplomats have noted in this connection that China is the only country from which Albania receives economic assistance. In their opinion the Chinese are aware that in the event of an estrangement with the Albanians, the influence of the USSR in the Balkans and in Europe will be strengthened even more.

Following the 7th Congress, the Albanian leaders and the country's mass communication media have been continuing to use any excuse for anti-Soviet attacks.

This was shown particularly clearly at the last session of Albania's National Assembly which confirmed the country's new constitution. Speeches about this by Hoxha, Lleshi, Nase, Hasbiu and other Albanian leaders were all of an anti-Soviet character.

Albania's policy towards the other countries of the Warsaw Pact will also essentially not change in the near future, according to the assessment of Western experts. At the same time they reckon that Albania is showing 'a differentiated approach' individual socialist countries.

In Western political circles the comment has been made that after the ALP Congress, at which Yugoslavia was subjected to serious attacks, the anti-Yugoslavia campaign in Albania was curtailed. This was brought about by the desire of the Albanian leadership to expand somewhat its contacts with neighbouring states which 'are not part of the zone of influence of the social-imperialists' [i.e. the Soviet Union]

Many Western experts point to the warming of Albania's relations with some capitalist countries like Italy, France, Belgium, Norway and Sweden. At the end of 1976 at a conference in the FRG Ministry of Foreign Affairs a proposal was formulated 'to begin a dialogue with Albania over its demands for reparations for the damage wrought on the country by fascist Germany'. Within the FRG Ministry of Foreign Affairs it is assumed that this 'will provide the opportunity to draw' Albania into a dialogue with the FRG and NATO on other questions as well. Greece is resolutely striving for the establishment of closer contacts between Albania and the West. As the Greek Minister of Foreign Affairs Bitsios recently declared, the aim of Greek policy is to

convince Albania that she will gain by drawing closer to the other
Balkan countries and to the West.

If opportunities present themselves in the future please despatch to
the Centre any additional intelligence about the questions touched on
above.

IRTYSHOV.

[Y.A. SHISHKIN

Deputy Head, FCD]

The cooling of Sino-Albanian relations proceeded more rapidly
than the Centre had anticipated. In the summer of 1977 a series
of Tirana newspaper articles accused China of 'opportunism'
and 'flagrant departures from the teachings of Marxism–
Leninism'.[11] Albania now proclaimed itself in effect the only
genuine Marxist–Leninist state and the centre of world revolution. The Centre saw no alternative but to wait patiently for the
demise of Enver Hoxha and a change in Albanian leadership.

The Vatican

Until the early 1970s the KGB was far more interested in the Catholic Church within the Soviet Union than in the policy of the Vatican. Those most active in operations against the Church were provincial KGBs in the main Catholic areas – the Ukraine, Byelorussia and Lithuania – who sent regular reports to the Fifth Directorate in Moscow, founded in 1968 to monitor dissent and 'ideological subversion' in all its forms. During the 1970s the FCD began to take a more active interest in the Vatican. Residencies were asked, on a number of occasions, to supply intelligence on what the Centre believed were the Papacy's increasingly subversive contacts with Soviet Catholics. Their reports were passed on to provincial KGBs.[12]

At the end of the decade the main focus of the Centre's concern with Catholic 'subversion' moved to Poland. It was severely shaken by the mushroom growth in 1980–81 of Polish Solidarity, led by an unemployed electrician, Lech Walesa, who began each day at Mass. Polish experts in the FCD traced the origins of the Solidarity 'crisis' back to the election in October 1978 of the Polish Cardinal Carol Wojtyla as Pope John Paul II. The moral authority of Poland's Communist government was visibly eclipsed by that of the Polish Pope. John Paul II's triumphal tour of Poland in 1979 witnessed an outpouring of national and religious emotion unparalleled since the Second World War. The Centre was better aware than most Western experts that the military coup ably executed by General Wojcieck Jaruzelski in December 1981 with the blessing of the FCD had achieved only a temporary halt in the onward march of 'ideological subversion'. When the Pope returned to Poland to another hero's welcome in 1983, he urged those who opposed the regime to turn to the Church for protection. In October 1984 the Polish Church gained a new martyr when the SB (the Polish security service) abducted and murdered the pro-Solidarity

priest, Father Jerzy Popielusko. Walesa declared at his grave-
side: 'Solidarity is alive because you have given your life for it'.[13]

By now, the days were long past when any Soviet leader was
tempted to repeat Stalin's scornful question, 'How many divi-
sions has the Pope?' The FCD 'Plan of Work' for 1984 named the
Papacy as a priority target. The Vatican, claimed the Centre, was
out to subvert the Soviet Bloc in the belief that 'the action of the
Polish Church to strengthen its position in the state can be
extended to other socialist countries'. The Pope's next two
targets, it concluded, were Hungary and Yugoslavia. In December 1984 the Centre sent out a major directive calling for more
intelligence on the Vatican's 'subversive activity', and for 'large-
scale active measures' to discredit John Paul II personally, create
dissension within the Catholic Church, and weaken its authority.
For these operations to succeed, however, more agents were
required – 'above all, in the Vatican'.

Vn-1   No 733
No. 2182/PR   Top Secret
19.12.84   Copy No 1
                                                                     To RESIDENTS

WORK ON THE VATICAN

In recent years the Head of the Catholic Church and right-wing circles
in the Vatican have been stepping up subversive activity against the
socialist countries and the national liberation and anti-war movements.

In view of this, the heads of our Department attach great importance
to more active efforts on the part of our organization abroad to
penetrate, using agents or other operational means, into the leading
Catholic centres of the West in order to obtain intelligence about
hostile operations in preparation by the Vatican, and also to carry out
large-scale active measures directed towards inciting prominent figures
in the Catholic Church to protest in defence of peace and limitation of
the arms race.

In consideration of the idea put forward by the Vatican for creating
under the banner of a so-called 'religious international', an inter-

national alliance to combat communist ideology, we think it expedient to step up operational work with agents in the clerical circles of the country where you are stationed, in order to deal with the tasks set by the heads of our Department and Service for working against the Vatican.

Attachment: Guidelines on measures to counteract the subversive activity of the Vatican. Top Secret, Copy No 11, 5 pages, No 12ss PN

SVETLOV
[GRIBIN]

[ms note]
Comrade GORNOV [GORDIEVSKY] and
PR Line operational staff
Lavrov 26.XII.84

Top Secret
Copy No II

Attachment to No 2182/PR
of 19 December 1984

Measures to counter the subversive activity of the Vatican

In recent times, as the ideological battle in the international arena has been sharply intensified, the Vatican has pursued a policy of more energetic subversive action by the Catholic Church in socialist countries, converting a religious movement into a political opposition force.

The anti-socialist bias of the Vatican's activity has become particularly marked with the arrival on the papal throne of John Paul II, whose hostility towards the countries of the socialist community is conditioned both by his personal anti-communist and anti-Soviet convictions and by the influence exerted on him by the most conservative representatives of the Catholic clergy and reactionary political figures of the West, especially those of the USA.

The views of the present Vatican hierarchy have found expression in a document published recently with the Pope's approval, entitled 'Comments on some aspects of liberation theology', which contains some sharp pronouncements about the socialist countries. Marxist doctrine is declared to be incompatible with the Christian faith, and the struggle of those nations fighting for their political, social and spiritual liberation is regarded as inadmissible.

The Pope and his entourage are endeavouring by every possible means to change the established relationship between church and state in the socialist countries. In the light of the 'Polish experience', they are trying in the first place to obtain actual complete independence of the church from the state, strengthen the position of reactionary clergy in the socialist countries and intensify anti-socialist feeling among the Catholic clergy and faithful.

The Vatican is at present putting the main emphasis in its so-called 'Eastern policy' on practical steps to revive the activity of Catholic and Uniate parishes, and on material and spiritual support for the most reactionary priesthood, inspiring and propagating negative attitudes among the faithful and setting up an organized 'religious opposition' to pursue the aim of strengthening the church's influence on the social and political processes in the socialist countries.

Steps are being taken by the Vatican to pursue this strategic line using both legal and illegal forms of operation. These are reinforced by widespread propaganda campaigns accusing the socialist countries of violating the provisions of the 'Final Act' of the All-European Conference, concerning 'religious freedom' and 'human rights'.

In leading circles in the Vatican, the Catholic Church is considered to be the sole, well-organized, legal opposition institution capable of exerting an influence on the broad masses, including workers and young people, and they calculate that the tactics they have recently adopted may lead to destabilization of the political situation in certain states of the socialist community, or in some parts of the Soviet Union.

The Vatican also assumes that the action of the Polish Church to strengthen its position in the state can be extended to other socialist countries.

The Vatican is seen to be active, too, in strengthening the positions of the Catholic Church in the Christian churches' ecumenical movement. Many statements of heads of the Roman Curia contain appeals to various religions and churches to 'forget past feuds and achieve mutual understanding and co-operation in the fight against atheism'. In this respect particular attention should be paid to the Vatican's efforts to achieve an alliance with the Russian Orthodox Church and to establish contacts with the Georgian Orthodox, the Armenian–Gregorian and other churches, including Protestant ones, operating in socialist countries. The Vatican has proclaimed the idea of creating a so-called 'religious international' (including not only Christians, but also Islam) to combat communist ideology.

The Catholic Leadership is taking specific steps to create a 'catacomb' (illegal) church and ecumenical underground societies in socialist countries 'under the flag of ecumenism', and attempts are being made to erode the unity of individual churches, (for example the Russian Orthodox Church)* by bringing in the idea of 'twinned parishes' among different religious confessions of various countries and cities.

The Vatican is endeavouring to establish diplomatic relations with socialist states in order to secure wider opportunities for pursuing its planned policy. In the Pope's opinion his speeches in defence of peace and disarmament should arouse interest on the part of the governments of these countries in developing contacts with the 'Holy See'. At the same time the Vatican's principal interest is concentrated on the most 'promising' countries of Eastern Europe, from its point of view: Poland, Hungary and Yugoslavia. Vatican diplomacy attaches great importance to organizing trips by the Pope to East European countries and the Soviet Union, which in its estimation might help to further the growth of religious feeling among the population of the countries he visits. The Vatican is endeavouring to organize papal visits to Poland, Yugoslavia, Czechoslovakia and the Soviet Union.

The Vatican also pursues a reactionary policy in relation to progressive social and political forces. For instance, right-wing groups in the Vatican have recently considerably expanded their subversive activity against the national liberation movement, above all in Latin America.

Prominent reactionary Catholics, in active co-operation with the leaders of the chief NATO countries, are endeavouring, with the Pope's approval, to weaken the anti-war movement. John Paul II and his supporters in the Vatican are trying to prevent Catholics and Catholic organizations from being involved in this movement.

In view of what has been said, the efforts of the intelligence service abroad must be directed to obtaining information on the following main points:

- the plans, forms and methods of subversive activity on the part of the Vatican and churches and organizations under its control against the countries of the socialist community and national liberation and anti-war movements;
- any action by the Roman Curia to strengthen the position of the

---

* RPT [Russkaya Pravoslavnaya Tserkov] in the original KGB text

Catholic Church in the states of the socialist community and turn it into a political force to oppose the socialist system;
- the attitude of the Pope and his immediate entourage in regard to the following grave, topical, international questions: East-West dialogue, political and military détente, the arms race, disarmament, etc;
- the Vatican's relations with the larger countries of the capitalist world and the PRC; co-ordination of policy and co-operation, especially with the United States and other NATO countries, in undermining the position of socialism and the national liberation and anti-war movements, including also co-operation with their special services;
- Vatican action to expand and strengthen the influence of Catholism in the developing countries of Asia, Africa and Latin America;
- the situation in the Roman Curia: the disposition of forces and the struggle for influence between the various trends and groupings.

Work on active measures must be pursued in the following directions:

- discrediting specific manifestations of hostile activity on the part of the Vatican against the socialist countries. Conveying to the leading groups of the Roman Curia and to John Paul II personally, the information that demands for expansion of the sphere of action of the Catholic Church within the social and state system in socialist countries is regarded by them as interference in their internal affairs and may in consequence lead to deterioration of relations between the state and the church, and also between the socialist countries and the Vatican;
- exploiting, in the interests of the socialist countries, the existence of any internal dissensions in the Vatican, any dissatisfaction ascertained on the part of influential cardinals with what is, in their opinion, the 'excessive enthusiasm' of Pope John Paul II for his 'Eastern policy', to the detriment of other sectors of the Vatican's activity. Emphasizing the fact that lack of concentration on the problems of the Catholic Church and the broad mass of the faithful in Western countries and many topical international questions may, in the final account, affect the authority of the Vatican;
- inspiring appeals from Catholic circles to John Paul and the Roman Curia to make a contribution to the cause of strengthening peace and international security, stopping the arms race, cutting down

military expenditure and using the resources thus released for the fight against hunger and poverty, for solving the problem of unemployment and providing aid for the developing countries, and for other humanitarian purposes;

– countering the expansion of contacts between the Vatican and the Russian Orthodox, Georgian, Armenian–Gregorian and other Christian churches, which are active in socialist countries, and its efforts to make use of these contacts in its own interests;

– exposing attempts by the Roman Curia to promote the anti-social activity of reactionary elements in Catholic and Uniate circles in the territory of socialist countries and plans to make use of the church as a weapon for ideological sabotage of the socialist system in these countries;

– carrying out measures to counter the establishment of a world organization of young Catholics;

– reinforcing the negative view taken by senior Catholic personalities regarding certain aspects of John Paul II's foreign policy and his interpretation of Catholicism. In particular, making use of dissatisfaction among Italian members of the Roman Curia with the Pope's intention of strengthening his own position by promoting Poles, West Germans and other non-Italians in the Catholic hierarchy;

– taking steps to discredit John Paul II as the protégé of the most reactionary circles in the West, and exposing his anti-communist and anti-Soviet aims. Undertaking measures to counteract his attempts to push the Catholic Church into confrontation with the countries of the socialist camp;

– discrediting the policy of right-wing groups in the Vatican designed to undermine the national liberation and anti-war movements;

– uncovering and exposing co-operation between representatives of the Vatican and organizations of the Catholic Church, and the CIA and the special [intelligence] services of NATO countries;

In order to deal with these tasks, steps must be taken to make more systematic use of existing agent resources and to create new ones in Catholic centres and organizations and, above all, in the Vatican.

The Arctic, the Antarctic and the World's Oceans

In the mid-1970s the Arctic emerged for the first time as a major KGB concern. The deployment of Delta Class submarines armed with ICBMs in 1973 gave the Soviet Union the capacity for the first time to launch a nuclear attack on the United States from the Barents Sea. The Centre believed that growing Western interest in the oil and natural gas deposits of Spitzbergen and the rest of the Svalbard archipelago posed a major strategic threat. Western oil-rigs, it feared, would be equipped to monitor the movements of the submarines and surface ships of the Soviet Northern Fleet. Moscow also saw the long drawn-out international negotiations on the Law of the Sea which began in 1974 as a potential threat to Soviet claims to the continental shelf beneath the Barents Sea. These concerns led to the creation of the winter of 1975–6 of a Soviet Interministerial Commission on the Arctic chaired by N.A. Tikhonov, First Deputy Prime Minister, with Kryuchkov as one of its key members.

Intelligence collection on Norway and the Arctic was now considered of such vital importance that it was personally supervised by the Chairman of the KGB, Yuri Andropov. The Centre's most important source was Arne Treholt, the Norwegian under-secretary responsible for the Law of the Sea negotiations. During Norwegian–Soviet negotiations in 1977 on the delimitation of the Barents Sea, Treholt not only kept the KGB fully informed of the Norwegian negotiating position but also acted as a Soviet agent of influence.[14] In April 1978 the Centre issued a major directive 'On the Activities of the West in the Arctic'. 'At the present time', it told Residents, 'the military-strategic, political and economic interests of the Soviet Union demand the adoption of all-embracing measures to reinforce its physical presence and juridical rights in the Arctic'. Though the Centre disliked Norway's fisheries conservation policy, it hoped that on other issues of Arctic policy it would be able to play off Norway against other Western powers. The April directive ended by emphasizing the 'great importance' which the Politburo as well as the Centre attached to intelligence on Western plans in the Arctic region.

nm 6   Top Secret
No 2121/PR/52   Copy No 1
20 April 1978
                        To: Residents (according to list)

ON THE ACTIVITIES OF THE WEST IN THE ARCTIC

The ruling circles of the Imperialist Powers, especially the USA, have recently been making persistent efforts to strengthen their political, economic and military positions in those regions where previously no sharp confrontation between East and West had been discernible. Thus, the Arctic, by virtue of its growing economic and military-strategic importance, has been steadily attracting the attention of the West.

Prognoses concerning the presence in the Arctic regions of rich deposits of oil and gas together with the exploitation of the deposits in the North Sea have given powerful stimuli to the activities of various countries keen to take control over this region. The Arctic is also rich in foodstuffs which the West is beginning to regard as a strategic weapon in its global policy. The Arctic has also always been considered, from the military-strategic point of view, as a very important region since the shortest airspace routes between the USA and the USSR pass over its territories, and those seas of the Arctic Ocean which do not freeze over provide the sole means of access for ships of the Soviet Northern Fleet into the Atlantic Ocean. The Western Powers are actively opening up this theatre of military operations. This is made significantly easier by the fact that a broad-based infrastructure utilized by NATO already exists in some of the Arctic regions (Iceland, Greenland and Northern Norway).

In a preliminary report by a special EEC group, a zone between Greenland and Norway was designated as being a source of energy potential of the greatest future significance 'within the confines of the jurisdiction of the member states of the community'. The Western Powers are persistently trying to obtain Norwegian agreement to guarantee to the multinational companies access 'without discrimination' to the oil resources of the Norwegian continental shelf right up to the border with the USSR. In a closed conference held in Oslo in 1976 on problems connected with oil exploration and processing in the North, the US representative unequivocally stated that in the event of a new Arab boycott the Americans would set in motion all means at their disposal to guarantee maximum exploitation of the oil resources of the North Sea and the Arctic.

The Western Powers closely link their plans for economic exploitation of the Arctic with military-strategic considerations. In the sessions of bi-partite working groups on problems of the Arctic, the representatives of the Western Powers strive to convince the Norwegians that the activities of oil companies in the Barents Sea would make NATO more interested in defending Norway in crisis situations and would strengthen the position of that country in negotiations with the USSR.

The scientific research being carried out by the Western Powers also has military application. Thus, in the report of the American committee concerned with the organization of an ice-breaking expedition following Nansen's route which is planned for the spring of 1978, it was explained that one of the aims of the expedition was the 'detection of acoustic peculiarities which have to be taken into account for the development of equipment essential for underwater operations in the Arctic Ocean'. Apart from the Americans, the Swedes are also preparing for another expedition through the seas of the Arctic Ocean, in which it is proposed to repeat the voyage undertaken in this region by Nordenscheld.

Attempts by NATO countries to expand their activities to the Spitzbergen archipelago have been noticed; navigational stations have already been constructed linked up with the US aero-space communications system; also an aerodrome capable of use by jet aircraft; Spitzbergen is regularly visited by Norwegian warships and aircraft. The NATO leaders, using the pretext of keeping a check on fishing in the 200-mile economic zone off the Norwegian coastline and on the 200-mile fisheries conservation zone around Spitzbergen, have demanded from the Norwegians the construction of a special patrol fleet in order to keep track of Soviet warship and aircraft movements.

The absence of universally recognized, clear-cut statutes of international Marine Law determining the maritime boundaries of in-

dividual states creates favourable prerequisites for the Western Powers
to put forward the idea of the 'internationalization' of the Arctic; that
is to say, the acknowledgement of the total surface area of the seas
within the confines of the Soviet Arctic Sector as an 'open sea'. As is
evident from available data the Western Powers may put forward this
idea in case of a breakdown in the Soviet-Norwegian negotiations on
the demarcation of the continental shelf of the Barents Sea, and states
poor in energy resources together with developing countries may
support it. In the opinion of individual Western Powers the mere
formulation of such a proposition will be to the definite political
detriment of the Soviet Union.

In the course of their negotiations with the Soviet representatives the
Norwegians have stuck to the principle of the 'meridian line' (that is the
line of equal distance from basic points on the territories of contiguous
countries) on the issue of the demarcation of the continental shelf of the
Barents Sea, claiming thereby an area of more than 150,000 square
kilometres currently included in the Soviet Polar Sector. The
Norwegians have introduced a 200-mile fisheries conservation zone
around Spitzbergen, and this also includes a part of the Soviet Polar
Sector. These actions by the Norwegians are contrary to Soviet interests and, in fact, coincide with the general Western line on limiting the
Soviet Union's influence in the Arctic. At the same time the Norwegian
government is striving with all its powers to secure, physically and
juridically, extensive areas of the Polar regions, and this objectively
creates favourable conditions for bi-partite Soviet–Norwegian co-
operation, especially if account is taken of the fact that powerful
Western countries disagree with Norway on various aspects of its
policies in the Arctic. Apart from this the Norwegians are interested in
maintaining a 'traditionally low level of tension in Northern Europe'.

In its efforts against the advancement of the idea of 'internationalization' of the Arctic, the Soviet Union can also, to a certain extent, count
on the support of Canada, which despite pressure from its allies still
favours points of view close to those of the USSR on the problems of the
Arctic. The Canadians have come out in favour of the sectoral principle
in the demarcation of the continental shelf, full national sovereignty
over its waters, navigable zones, straits and airspace, and Canadians
also favour strict conditions governing the exploration for, and processing of, valuable minerals. They are ready to agree only to the
discussion of topics connected with the security of navigation and
protection of the environment, but at the same time they consider that

only those countries with territories in the Arctic continental belt should take part in such discussions.

At the present time the military-strategic, political and economic interests of the Soviet Union demand the adoption of all-embracing measures to reinforce its physical presence and juridical rights in the Arctic. In this connection great importance is attached to the acquisition and submission to the Centre of up-to-date intelligence on the problems of the Arctic which is essential for the preparation and implementation of a complex of measures on the part of the Soviet Union in this region. Special attention must, therefore, be centred on obtaining reliable data on the plans and specific activities of the West in the Arctic, with a view to throwing light on the following topics in particular:

1. The discussion of military-political and economic questions concerning the Arctic within the NATO and EEC institutions, and also within the International Energy Agency. The positions of the participants, especially the Americans, Canadians, West Germans, Norwegians and Danes. Plans and possible steps adopted by the NATO leadership with relation to the Arctic regions aimed at undermining Soviet security. Intelligence on applied military research and completion of the NATO infrastructure in the Arctic. Divergencies in the positions of individual members of the bloc, including where these are conditioned by their specific national interests in the region.

2. Intelligence on the plans for the 'internationalization' of the Arctic which are being worked out by Western NATO member-countries. The juridical and political arguments supporting these intentions. The attitudes of individual countries (primarily the Americans, Norwegians, Danes and Canadians, but also the French and Japanese) to these plans. Possible specific steps on the part of the West towards officially launching these plans, with the aim of undermining the political position of the USSR, measures aimed at securing support on these issues on the part of neutral non-aligned and developing countries.

3. Data on the work of the mixed bi-partite working groups on the Arctic, composed of Norway and the USA, Britain, France and the FRG. The presence of other groups of a similar kind with Western countries participating. The basic topics discussed at sessions of these groups, the points of view of the various sides, the decisions and recommendations adopted and the results achieved (in the

opinion of those taking part). Information about the possibility of the West adopting a common stance with regard to the UN conference on the Law of the Sea.

4. Specific information on the direction, scope and future development of economic activity in the Arctic by the leading Western Powers.

5. The studies being carried out by scientific research institutions and by the ministries and departments responsible for them on problems connected with the exploitation of fuel-energy, mineral and foodstuffs resources of the Arctic: the facilities allotted to scientific research and experimental development work for this purpose. Specific plans and steps taken by the USA and Sweden for the implementation of projects to send maritime expeditions to the Arctic.

6. The attitudes of the principal Western Powers on Spitzbergen, their views regarding Norwegian measures to strengthen Norway's sovereignty over the archipelago and to the establishment of 'national' control in the zone surrounding it. The West's appraisal of the functioning of the 1920 Paris treaty on Spitzbergen. Problems of the Spitzbergen continental shelf and possible solutions, as envisaged by the Western countries.

7. The progress and results of prospecting work undertaken by the Norwegians in individual parts of Spitzbergen; intelligence on participation by foreign specialists.

8. Concrete examples of pressure by the West on Norway with a view to obtaining a tougher line *vis-à-vis* the Soviet Union with regard to the problems of the Arctic regions, including the resolution of problems which arise from the Soviet presence in Spitzbergen. The evaluation by Western countries, principally the USA, of the current policy of the Norwegian government towards these problems, any evidence that these countries are co-ordinating their policy towards Norway.

When organizing work on the problems of the Arctic, it is essential to bear in mind the long-term nature of this requirements and the great importance which the authorities* and also our department attach to the acquisition of intelligence on the topics indicated.

SEVEROV

[V F GRUSHKO]

[Head of the Third Department, FCD]

---

* *Instantsiya* in Russian. In KGB documents, this denotes the highest political leadership, specifically the Party Politburo.

There was no slackening over the next few years in the Centre's interest in the Arctic. In 1981 General Titov, then head of the Third Department which directed KGB operations in Scandinavia, proposed the establishment of a new Residency equipped with a sigint station at Barentsburg on Spitzbergen in order to monitor Norwegian activity and Western naval movements in the area. His proposal was approved in the winter of 1981–82. Simultaneously a new Arctic Section was founded in FCD Service 1 (Reports), headed by A.P. Semyonov who had previously been stationed at the KGB Residency in Stockholm.

The 'Plan for Work on the Problems of the World's Oceans, the Arctic and the Antarctic, 1982–1985' distributed to Residencies in December 1982 had comparatively little to say about intelligence requirements in the Arctic, probably because these were being so amply supplied by Treholt. Late in 1978 Treholt had been posted to the Norwegian mission to the United Nations, for part of his time in New York, Norway was a member of the Security Council. In 1982–83 he was at the Norwegian Defence College, cleared for NATO 'cosmic' top-secret material; the prosecutor at his trial later likened Treholt's activities in the college to those of a fox let loose on a chicken farm.[15]

The Centre felt much less well supplied with intelligence on the Oceans and the Antarctic which were listed for the first time in 1982 as KGB priority targets. Both the United States rapprochement with China and the Japanese economic miracle had strengthened the Soviet sense of vulnerability in the Pacific. The Centre's Work Plan identified three main specific anxieties: the role of submarine-launched nuclear missiles in alleged US and NATO plans for a first strike against the USSR; the implications of American refusal to ratify the UN Law of the Sea Convention; and United States schemes to exploit its superiority in deep-water technology by pressing ahead with the extraction of minerals from the seabed.

No 1967/PR   Top Secret
15.11.82   Copy No 1
                        To Residents

PLAN FOR WORK ON THE PROBLEMS OF THE WORLD'S OCEANS, THE
ARCTIC AND THE ANTARCTIC, 1982–1985

The heads of our department have endorsed our service's plan for
working on the problems of the world's oceans, the Arctic and
Antarctic for 1982–1985. These issues have been listed as priorities for
your Residency. Work in this field must therefore be embodied in the
structure of the plan and the results shown in annual reports.

The world's oceans, the Arctic and the Antarctic are acquiring
continually increasing global importance among the range of issues
involved in inter-state relations.

The American and NATO doctrine on military strategy envisages
wide use of naval forces, primarily underwater-based, as one of the
major forms of offensive strategic armaments and weapons for a 'first
strike' directed against the USSR.

At the same time, ensuring permanent access to the mineral
resources of the sea bed is considered by the USA to be of vital
importance for the economy and defence of the country. The Americans are preparing to expand their mastery of the oceans' resources,
reckoning on exploiting their leading position in this area as an
additional lever to exert influence on their allies and also on the
socialist and liberated countries.

The United States has refused to vote for adoption of the text of an
International Convention prepared by the third UN conference on the
Law of the Sea and has declared that it will not sign it. At the same time
it is confronting the socialist and developing countries with an
imperialist alternative solution for the matter, having concluded an
agreement in September this year with Britain, the FRG and France for
regulating temporarily the extraction of useful minerals in the open
sea. Our adversary is also maturing plans to implement practical
measures prejudicial to the interests of the USSR in the world's oceans,
the Arctic and the Antarctic.

At the same time the adoption of the International Convention does
not settle all questions. Problems such as the delimitation of territorial

waters, maritime economic zones and the continental shelf between contiguous countries continue to be of topical importance, as do also problems of economic exploitation in international waters.

The USSR is interested in peaceful, rational exploitation of the subsoil, seabed and expanse of the world's oceans and in arrangements for equal co-operation with all countries for mutually advantageous utilization of the mineral and organic resources of the sea.

Our service is also called upon to make its contribution towards solving these grave problems, pursuing its activity in the following principal directions:

1. Information-gathering and Analysis

Attention should be concentrated on obtaining covert information on the following matters:

- The military strategy of the USA and NATO in the world's oceans. Plans and specific measures of the NATO political and military leadership to strengthen its position in the most promising zones and areas for operational deployment of a naval strike force and underwater nuclear forces intended for attacking Soviet territory and blockading Soviet naval forces, especially in the North Atlantic, the Mediterranean basin and the northern waters of the Pacific and Indian Oceans.
- Intentions and the most important actions on the part of the USA, other developed capitalist countries and also states belonging to 'Group 77' in regard to entry into force and practical implementation of the international convention on the Law of the Sea. Attempts by the USA to use the separate agreement with Great Britain, the FRG and France to undermine the convention and inflict damage on Soviet interests.
- The growth of contradictions between the USA and the rest of the world on the problems of the world's oceans. American measures to increase their superiority in deep-water technology and control over strategic resources in order to exercise political influence. Any manoeuvres by large American companies to change their national flag in order to register sectors with the International Sea Bed Agency and the probable military and political consequences of this. Approaches by the USA to third countries to conclude bilateral and regional agreements on exploiting the continental shelf and economic zones of these countries.

- The national programmes for the world's oceans of Canada, Australia, and individual European countries (especially Great Britain, the FRG, France, Italy, Norway and the other Scandinavian countries); in Asia (primarily Japan, India, Indonesia); in Latin America (especially Mexico, Venezuela, Brazil, Argentina, Peru), and African countries. The prospects for co-operation between the USSR and specific countries abroad in military and economic spheres related to the world's oceans. Possible actions by the adversary damaging to Soviet interests.
- Any complications expected in the situation in individual areas in connection with the process of demarcation of territorial waters, the continental shelf and maritime economic zones. The competitive struggle on the issues of economic activity in international waters.
- The military and political concepts of the USA, Canada, Norway and Denmark in the Arctic and how they are implemented. The policy of these countries in the matter of carrying out provisions of the convention on the Law of the Sea on the jurisdiction of these states in areas covered by ice. Specific operations designed to 'internationalize' the Arctic. The 'Arctic' programmes of Japan, the FRG, Great Britain, France, and other Western countries and also China.
- Designs of individual countries, including members of 'Group 77' to extend the operation of the convention on the Law of the Sea to the Antarctic. Any plans designed to undermine the 1959 Antarctic Treaty to the detriment of the Soviet Union's interests. Any operations planned to make use of the territorial division of the Antarctic. American intentions regarding development of its natural resources.

2. Active Measures

The main tasks of our intelligence service abroad in this field are considered to be:

- Exposure of the United States' and NATO plans and activity to exploit the world's oceans for purposes of military strategy, and especially to create and build up military bases in particular maritime zones and areas and to concentrate surface and underwater nuclear forces with the intention of carrying out attacks on the USSR.
- Promotion of the signing and later on also the ratification of the

international convention of the Law of the Sea, by the majority of the States of the world.

- Exposing the policy of the USA and its principal allies designed to achieve unilateral advantages in opening up the world's oceans.
- Discrediting any attempts by the USA and other NATO countries to involve individual developing countries in exploiting specific resources of the sea bed in international areas, circumventing the international convention.
- Helping to deepen existing contradictions and differences between the USA and other countries of the world on questions related to the world's oceans.
- Exposing American ideas on politicizing the problems of the Arctic and 'internationalizing' areas of the Arctic.
- Helping to disrupt any plans designed to undermine the 1959 Antarctic Treaty to the detriment of the USSR's interests.
- Creating suitable conditions for importing modern deep-water equipment and technology into the USSR.

The following action must be taken to deal with the tasks mentioned:

Using the existing operational facilities, undertake action to promote the protection of the Soviet Union's interests in the matter of the world's oceans, and discredit United States' policy, especially attempts to create obstacles to the entry into force of the International Convention, and to 'internationalize' Arctic issues, etc.

Special emphasis must be put on exposing American plans to exploit the world's oceans for purposes of military strategy, especially in the north-western and north-eastern parts of the Pacific Ocean, areas of the Indian Ocean, the Persian Gulf, the Panama Canal and the Malacca Straits:

Work energetically to aggravate disagreements between the USA and industrially developed, and also developing, countries on a number of serious issues connected with the world's oceans. Utilize especially, in the interests of the USSR, the disagreement on the part of Canada and some other countries with the attitude of the USA on Arctic questions and the dissatisfaction of the liberated countries with American policy on exploiting the resources of the sea.

3. Operational Work with Agents

In order to carry out the tasks mentioned above in the fields of information and analysis, and of implementing influence operations, steps must be taken to exploit existing agent facilities to good purpose and to create new ones.

To this end:

- Determine the main targets (state institutions, involved in formulating and implementing policy in regard to the world's oceans, scientific research institutes and large firms connected with study of these matters, and with designing and producing the requisite equipment, and international organizations, etc) and organize planned study of these. Step up work on targets which have already been identified and persons of interest to us in these targets, in order to obtain information and samples of equipment, and also carry out influence operations.

- Examine the intelligence access of agents, confidential contacts and special unofficial contacts among foreign nationals and suggest specific sectors for employing them.

- Take steps to acquire new agents and confidential contacts among foreigners, above all from among civil servants, representatives of the business world, scientists, specialists, who have real prospects of carrying out assignments connected with world ocean problems.

- Select from among co-opted Soviet citizens persons who have suitable access by virtue of the position they occupy in Soviet institutions abroad, ministries and departments, scientific establishments or international organizations; supplement the range of co-opted Soviet citizens with the necessary specialists and experts on world ocean questions who are working in departments and scientific institutions (IMEMO, ISKAN, IKIAN,* the State and Law Institute, the Latin America Institute, etc). Pay particular attention to Soviet specialists working in international organizations concerned with world Ocean matters.

- Arrange for case officers, and also agents and persons of confidential status among Soviet citizens, to be sent to scientific centres and institutions in Western countries which are concerned with

---

* the Moscow State Institute for International Relations, the United States and Canada Institute, the Chinese Institute of the Academy of Sciences

oceanographic research, through scientific exchanges as members of delegations, trainees and post-graduate students.

SILIN
[G F TITOV]
[Head of the Third Department, FCD]

Despite the growing importance of the Pacific in Soviet strategy during the early 1980s, the KGB presence in Australasia remained small: only seven legal officers in Australia and even fewer in New Zealand. Jubilation in Moscow over the election of David Lange's Labour government in New Zealand on an anti-nuclear programme in 1984, however, led to plans to expand KGB operations. The Centre told the London Residency that it attached 'huge importance' to operations designed to organize European support for Lange's anti-nuclear policies. KGB officers were promised decorations if they succeeded in gaining influence over any anti-nuclear movement (Greenpeace excepted because of its 'anti-Soviet' line on whaling).[16]

Greater KGB optimism in the Pacific was balanced by a major setback in Arctic intelligence collection. On 20 January 1984 Arne Treholt was arrested in Oslo as he was about to board a plane for a rendezvous in Vienna with Gennadi Titov, head of the FCD Third Development. In his briefcase were 66 classified documents from the Norwegian Foreign Ministry.[17] For more than a year (perhaps longer), the KGB Residency in London had received no telegrams containing specific intelligence requirements on the Arctic. Following Treholt's arrest, it received five such telegrams in six weeks. The fifth, signed by Kryuchkov himself, quoted a recent analysis by the Centre of Arctic Intelligence which concluded that insufficient information was now being obtained, and exhorted the Residency to increase its efforts.

Africa

In the mid-1970s the Centre was full of optimism at the spread of Soviet influence in sub-Saharan Africa. A vaguely Marxist military junta, the Derg, seized power in Ethiopia in 1974. A year later the Marxist Front for the Liberation of Mozambique (FRELIMO) also emerged victorious. In 1976 the Marxist Popular Movement for the Liberation of Angola (MPLA), headed by Samora Machel, was recognized by the Organization for African Unity (OAU) as the legitimate government of Angola.

A decade later, the mood at the Centre had changed dramatically. It was taken by surprise in March 1984 when FRELIMO signed the Nkomati non-aggression agreement with South Africa.[18] Soon afterwards N.V. Shishlin, foreign affairs consultant to the International Department (and later to Gorbachev), told the London Embassy and KGB Residency in a private briefing that 'saving Mozambique' was beyond Moscow's power; its economy had virtually collapsed and FRELIMO was riven with internal rivalries. Shishlin considered Angola's economic problems as catastrophic, and its political leadership as divided and incompetent, as those of Mozambique. He feared that the MPLA, like FRELIMO, might be forced to come to terms with South Africa.[19]

Telegrams from the Centre expressed similar concerns, usually in more guarded terms. Gordievsky noted (but did not copy) one telegram on Southern Africa, received by the London Residency shortly after Shishlin's briefing, which claimed that South Africa had been able to exploit the very difficult economic and political situation in various African states, particularly Angola and Mozambique, to pressurize them into agreements which were favourable to Pretoria. At the same time, the Centre believed, South Africans had their own economic problems and were finding it expensive to maintain garrisons in Southern Angola and Namibia, as well as supporting UNITA (Union for the

Total Liberation of Angola) and the Mozambique counter-
revolutionaries. This gave them an added incentive to reach a
settlement. The telegram implied that these developments already posed a threat to Soviet influence in the area and that this
threat might become serious.

The London Residency was asked for information on the following points:

a. US plans to undermine the Soviet position in Southern Africa;
b. US activity to pressurize its allies not to give more economic
   assistance to Angola and Mozambique;
c. South African attempts to emerge from isolation and to establish
   diplomatic relations with African states;
d. Western pressure on African states to support Western policy with
   regard to South Africa;
e. a possible move by Mozambique into the Western sphere of
   influence and possible preparations for a Mozambique rejection of
   military co-operation with the Soviet Union; the likelihood of
   Mozambique mediation between UNITA and the MPLA; Machel's
   position on the question of a Namibia settlement and the presence
   of Cuban troops in Angola; possible changes in FRELIMO's ideological base;
f. disagreements within the Angolan and Mozambique leaderships on
   possible reconciliation with their counter-revolutionary movements; the normalization of relations with South Africa and the
   USA as a means of neutralizing these movements; and the solution
   of their financial and economic crises. Which personalities within
   the leaderships were the main 'transmitters' of Western influence?
g. possible changes in the SWAPO position on a Namibian settlement
   and their readiness to reach a compromise. Which political organizations might stand against SWAPO in elections held under
   UN auspices?
h. the position of the African National Congress (ANC); Western
   attempts to dissolve the ANC or weaken its Marxist base; how
   serious were the statements by ANC representatives that they
   would carry on the struggle from Mozambique in spite of the treaty
   with South Africa?

Asia

The KGB's main Asian target was the People's Republic of China (PRC), which ranked immediately behind the United States and its NATO allies in the order of KGB global priorities.[20] Because of tight security within the PRC, however, Hong Kong became a more important base than Beijing for Line K (anti-Chinese) operations. Hong Kong contained, in addition to a number of PRC official missions, a wide variety of Beijing-controlled Hong Kong businesses and organizations, all of which were potential targets. In April 1978 the Centre sent Residents a list of PRC-controlled Hong Kong organizations, and other undertakings in Hong Kong with contacts in mainland China. Additional targets included foreign missions in Hong Kong, British and American intelligence agencies, and scientific institutions whose students were regarded as potential agents.

Some of the potential targets were shrewdly chosen. But there were also some curious omissions. Among 'the best informed' Hong Kong newspapers, the FCD made no mention of the *Ming Po*, considered by some Western Sinologists to be the best informed of all. The Centre's knowledge of Western intelligence operations was also curiously patchy. It referred to 'the RAF Radio Intercept Service' but made no mention of the important GCHQ signals intelligence (sigint) operations. Nor did it include in its long list of targets the Joint Services Intelligence Bureau and the Ministry of Defence Language School.

vm.1   SECRET
No 1734/PR/62   Copy No 1
20 April 1978

To Residents

We are forwarding herewith a brief on 'Basic targets of interest to line in Hong Kong' for your active consideration and possible operational utilization.

In our opinion this brief may be utilized in the organization of work against line 'K' targets from within third countries, in particular, in the implementation of operations designed to achieve the infiltration of our agents into Hong Kong.

Chinese Peoples' Republic (PRC) targets in Hong Kong

Although it retains its formal status as a colony, Hong Kong is, at the same time, fully within the sphere of Peking's* activities, both in the area of active foreign policy and economics. The influence of China on the internal life and external relations of Hong Kong is steadily increasing. The bulk of the PRC's foreign trade transactions are implemented through Hong Kong, so too is China's economic and scientific-technical co-operation with the outside world Hong Kong occupies an important place in the PRC's foreign tourism and also in the field of its overseas cultural relations. In the political sphere Hong Kong has been used, and continues to be used by the Chinese leadership, for establishing relations with Western countries. Hong Kong remains to this day the place where the Chinese prefer to contact their foreign partners using various methods including secret ones. As before, Hong Kong provides the connecting link between the PRC and the Chinese émigré communities in South East Asia and other regions of the world.

Because of all these factors there has been a marked increase in the number of PRC official missions in Hong Kong over the past few years and, equally, of various local organizations and undertakings which are under the control of Peking. Thus, the PRC controls more than 40 Hong Kong banks, a large number of trading and industrial firms, together with a number of local newspapers. Chinese influence is also strong in the Hong Kong trades-unions. Among the most important PRC official missions and local organizations controlled by Peking are the following:

- *The Bank of China*, 2A, Des Voeux Rd. C. Hong Kong; telephone 5–234191; telegraphic address *Chun Kuo Hong Kong.*
- *The China Travel Service H.K. Ltd*, 3 Queen's Rd. C. Hong Kong;

---

* Russian transliteration from Chinese corresponds to the traditional English method rather than the modern Pin-Yin (Peking, not Beijing).

telephone 5–224181–9; telegraphic address *Travelbank Hong Kong*. This agency deals with all questions concerning travel to the PRC by foreigners.

– *The Chinese General Chamber of Commerce*, 24 Connaught Rd. C. Hong Kong; telephone 5–2242555; telegraphic address *Chichacom, Hong Kong*. The Chamber ensures contacts between Peking and the representatives of overseas countries on various matters, supplying the Chinese with information on the state of the international markets.

– *The New China News Agency*, 5 Sharp Street, Hong Kong; telephone 5–720190; telegraphic address *Hsinhua, Hong Kong*.

– *The Hong Kong Chinese Clerks' Association*, 87 Lockhart Road, Hong Kong; telephone 4–729459.

– *The Hong Kong Federation of Trades Unions*.

– The Publishers of the newspaper *Ta Kung Pao*, 342, Hennessy Road, Hong Kong; Telephone H–728211.

– The Publishers of the newspaper *Wen Wei Pao*, 4 Percival Street, Hong Kong; telephone H–770923.

– *The China Resources Company*, Bank of China Building 2A Des Voeux Road, Hong Kong.

Business organizations in Hong Kong which maintain permanent contact with China

Hong Kong is the large financial, commercial and industrial centre of Asia. New firms are registered in Hong Kong at a rate of about 400 monthly. Bank investments there double themselves every five years. More than a million people visit Hong Kong each year, of whom 30–40 per cent are businessmen.

Hong Kong continues to be the main market for Chinese goods. The annual export of goods from the PRC to Hong Kong amounts to about 500 million US dollars. Hong Kong is one of the most important sources of foreign exchange for the PRC – more than 25 per cent.

The growth of business activity in Hong Kong, and the expansion of its ties with the PRC obliges local and foreign businessmen to devote greater attention to the study of the state of the economic market in China, and associated questions such as the situation in the PRC, the internal and external policy of the Chinese leadership, etc. There are a number of business organizations in Hong Kong, which concern themselves with collecting up-to-date information on the above-mentioned questions. Frequently this information is of a confidential nature. The following are among the more notable organizations of this type:

- *The Commerce and Industry Department*, Fire Brigade Building, Connaught Road Central, Hong Kong. This is a State organization concerned with matters relating to the trade and industry of the Colony. It is staffed by more than 1500 employees. In the Department's information office there is an index of about 10,000 subjects with information on various economic questions. This organization is one of the best sources for information on the PRC, covering a wide range of subjects.
- *The Federation of Hong Kong Industries*, ELDEX Industrial Building, 21 Ma Ta Wei Road, Hunghom, Kowloon. Founded in 1960, it aims at quality control and the observance of international standards for products manufactured in Hong Kong. The Federation has a good technical library. It makes recommendations to the government and private individuals on industrial matters and the setting up of new companies.
- *The Hong Kong General Chamber of Commerce*, 901–907 Union House, Chater Road, Hong Kong. Founded in 1861 – the first Hong Kong Chamber of Commerce. It has good sources of information on a variety of trade matters. There are more than two thousand member-companies in the Chamber representing banking, insurance, maritime affairs and all aspects of commercial activity. It has more than 75 employees including émigrés from the PRC. The Chamber of Commerce possesses one of the best commercial libraries in Hong Kong. This Chamber represents the UN office of EKADV* in Hong Kong and is a member of the *British National Chamber of Commerce* and the *Federation of British and Commonwealth Chambers of Commerce*. The office of the organization is to be found at Room 1128, Star House, Kowloon, Hong Kong.
- *The Chinese Manufacturers' Association*, CMA Building, 10th Floor, 64–65 Connaught Road Central, Hong Kong. Founded in 1934. More than 2,000 commercial firms are members. The Association has a permanent exhibition centre for displaying the products of member-companies. The organization may serve as a good intermediary for commercial contacts in the PRC and Hong Kong.

---

*This may be a garbled reference to the Bangkok-based ECAFE organization.

- *The American Chamber of Commerce,* 322 Edinburgh House, Hong Kong. Founded in 1969 for the development of trading relations between Hong Kong and the USA. It has more than 525 companies on its books and most of these have been founded in Hong Kong during the past few years. It has good trading contacts with the PRC and publishes interesting statistical reports and analytical material on trade with the PRC. Its permanent staff is not large. It has a library.
- *The Japanese Chamber of Commerce,* Queen's Road Central, Hong Kong. Founded to foster business contacts between Japan and Hong Kong. There are more than 4000 Japanese businessmen in Hong Kong and the Chamber of Commerce maintains close relations with most of these through its 120 member-companies.
- *Webb Associates Ltd,* PO Box 757, A-3 Gardena Court, 2 Kennedy Terrace, H.K. This is one of the best sources of information on the financial position and credit worthiness of Hong Kong companies. Apart from this, the firm specializes in the study of probable investors and also in the preparation of surveys on industry and trade.
- *The Hong Kong Exporters Association,* Star House, 6th Floor, Kowloon. It has 118 member-companies and files with information on a large number of companies. It is concerned with questions relating to the quality of goods produced in Hong Kong, and also on marine freightage. Although the number of member-companies is not large, they include some of the biggest in Hong Kong. The Association's information may be of value in checking the reputations of dubious companies.
- *The Trade Development Council,* Connaught Centre, Connaught Road Central, Hong Kong. A government organization concerned with the problems of export development and also economic and trade research. It has offices in London, New York, Chicago, Los Angeles, Toronto, Sydney, Tokyo, Amsterdam, Brussels, Frankfurt, Vienna, Manchester, Stockholm and Hamburg. It publishes a monthly journal, *Hong Kong Enterprise,* which is distributed gratis among 45,000 businessmen the world over. It is the only organization in Hong Kong which collects information on all business matters in Hong Kong.
- *The Chinese General Chamber of Commerce,* 24–25 Connaught Road Central, Hong Kong. Founded in 1900, it has 2000 member-companies and is the largest Chamber of Commerce in Hong Kong.

It maintains a pro-Peking attitude and is concerned in the commercial transactions between the PRC and foreign firms. It maintains
close contact with the Canton trade fair and also with State Trade
organizations in Peking and their representatives in Hong Kong.
– *The Kowloon Chamber of Commerce*, 2 Liberty Avenue, Kowloon.
  It has a membership of 40 companies and more than 3000 private
  persons whose interests are closely linked with Taiwan.
– *The Indian Chamber of Commerce*, 5a Duddell Street, Hong Kong.
  300 member-companies. This organization may be utilized for the
  collection of information on the PRC.

Foreign Missions in Hong Kong

The foreign policy departments of the Western countries and those of
the majority of developing countries regard Hong Kong as a highly
advantageous point from which to observe events in China. There are
35 Consulates-General in Hong Kong working independently from
either their embassies in Britain or in the PRC. The collection and
analysis of intelligence on the PRC is the main function of their staffs of
whom a large number are Chinese speakers.

There is always a very significant number of foreign journalists in
Hong Kong. Practically all the large Western press-organs, together
with those of the developing countries, are represented by their own
staff in Hong Kong. There are likewise many China specialists among
these foreign newsmen.

The US Consulate-General is the largest of all these foreign missions
in Hong Kong – its staff consists of 150 Americans and 400 locally
engaged citizens. The number of China specialists alone amounts to
approximately 60. Some of these were, before the formation of the
PRC, working in China.

The Consulate-General monitors the Chinese Press and reports
emerging from the PRC. It maintains a unique card-index on state and
political figures, party officials, academics, military and other personalities in the PRC whose names have appeared in the Chinese Press
or in other material.

Of particular interest is the Consulate-General's Department of
Continental China whose staff is directly concerned with the problems
of the PRC, in particular with the collection and analysis of intelligence
on political, economic and military matters, and with forecasting
developments and events in the PRC. The Department participates
directly in preparing the bulletin issued by the US Information Service

in Hong Kong, 'Current Scene'. In the editorial articles appearing in 'Current Scene' (whose authors are, as a rule, members of the Department) use is made of information on the PRC which has been obtained from intelligence sources.

On the subject of foreign journalists in Hong Kong (in the context of acquiring useful contacts and information on China) the following is worthy of attention: *The Foreign Correspondents Club of Hong Kong*, Sutherland Street; telephone 237734. Of the local Hong Kong newspapers, the best informed on the Chinese scene are the *South China Morning Post* and the *Hong Kong Standard*.

British Special [Intelligence] Service Sub-sections in Hong Kong

The Special Services of a number of Western countries are active in Hong Kong. Their main function is to obtain by all possible means intelligence on the situation in the CPR. The most active are the Special Services of Britain and the USA which frequently co-ordinate their activities on China. The British Special Services, being a part of the administrative set-up in Hong Kong, also fulfil counter-intelligence functions; they work in this connection partly from an official standpoint, which to some extent makes it easier to study them.

– Special Section of British Military Intelligence in Hong Kong. This is a small group of officers attached to the Defence Department. Among their tasks is the collection of intelligence of a military nature on the PRC including that obtained by way of exchanges with the Military Liaison Department of the American Consulate-General.
– The RAF radio intercept station in *Saiwan*. This is concerned with intercepting communications of a military nature in Southern China.
– The RAF monitoring station in the *Tui Mo Shan* region, New Territories.
– *Special Branch of the Hong Kong Police – SB*; telephone H-234011. This is the principal C.I organ of Hong Kong. This Department collates all available data on foreigners and organizes the work of studying them, paying particular attention to representatives of the socialist countries. The immigration section for checking bona fides, and the foreigners' registration section, are subordinate to this Department. The foreigners' registration section is responsible for refugees arriving in Hong Kong from China

illegally, while the Immigration section deals with Chinese immigrants who have exit visas from the PRC. The Special Branch maintains contact with, and assists local and foreign organizations; it also aids private individuals. For example, at the request of the American authorities it carries out a check of Chinese seeking entry visas to the USA. It is known that the Special Branch fulfils individual assignments on behalf of the FBI and communicates essential information to some of the better-known journalists.

– *The UK Regional Information Office for South-East Asia*, 501, Ridley House, 2 Upper Albert Road, Hong Kong; telephone H-234830. The R. I. O. is an analytical department of the British Foreign Office. It maintains contact with British Intelligence, and makes use of such sources as the résults of the BBC monitoring service, the correspondence of British Diplomats in Peking, the Hong Kong Police Special Branch reports on the results of interrogations of Chinese refugees and British Foreign Office material. The Weekly Bulletin of the R.I.O. – *China News Summary* – is distributed in English and Chinese to all the Hong Kong newspapers and to foreign Consulates-General, journalists and academics. In addition the R.I.O. distributes unofficially the publications of the Analysis Department of the British Foreign Office – *Asian Analyst, China Topics* and *China Notes*.

– *The BBC Monitoring Service*. This is a comparatively small group handling the intercept of the broadcasts of 12 Chinese provincial radio-stations. For technical reasons the BBC Hong Kong group is limited to Central, Southern and Western China. (The intercepting of broadcasts from Northern and North Eastern China is carried out by CIA's information service on Okinawa.) The intercepted information is made available on a commercial basis to journalists in Hong Kong and is then placed in the publication *Summary of World Broadcasts* which is issued daily by the Headquarters of the BBC Monitoring Service at Reading (England), Information obtained officially from the 'Hsinhua' agency is also included in this publication. The *Summary* is one of the most important sources on China for West European sinologues.

Hong Kong Scientific Institutions

From the operational point of view the most interesting Hong Kong Scientific Institutions are those that carry out research on Chinese subject matter and prepare students to become specialist scholars on

China. These have up-to-date information on China; and from among
their students may be found useful contacts including candidates for
deep study with future potential.

– *The Union Research Institute*, 9 College Road, Kowloon. This
  Institute was founded in 1951 and its Director is a Chinese – V. Sui,
  who is a specialist on Culture and Education in China. It is
  subsidized through the Asiatic Fund by the British government
  together with certain US monopolies. Its basic task is to make up-
  to-date information on China available to government, business
  and scientific circles in the USA and Western Europe. Fifty Americans, British and Chinese work in the Institute. There is a Secretariat, library and a research department which analyses incoming
  material. As sources of information it utilizes the press, television,
  Chinese films from the People's Republic, the reports of diplomats,
  businessmen, tourists and merchant seamen who visit China. The
  Institute publishes *China Weekly, China Monthly, Biographical
  Service* (biographical information on politicians and statesmen in
  the PRC). In addition to this it also publishes reference material,
  collections of documents on the history and economics of China, on
  military and political matters, on the activities and speeches of
  Chinese leaders etc.
– *The Universities Service Centre*, 155 Argyle Street, Kowloon;
  telephone K-640241. This forms part of the Union Research Institute. Created in 1963 with funds from the Carnegie and Ford
  foundations in order to assist Sinologues in the collection of
  essential information. The Centre maintains links with the US
  Consulate-General in Hong Kong and assists scholars from abroad
  to find suitable contacts in Hong Kong academic circles. Scientific
  workers and doctoral candidates, mainly Americans, come to the
  Centre to complete their theses. The Centre ensures possibilities for
  various categories of scientific-research work for young specialists
  in Chinese studies.
– *The Centre of Asian Studies, University of Hong Kong*. Its director
  is the American scholar, F. King, Professor of Economic History.
  The Centre is concerned with the study of Chinese history, philosophy and culture, together with the Chinese language and the
  political and economic problems of contemporary China. In recent
  years the Centre has regularly organized scientific conferences and
  symposia on various Chinese and East Asian subjects. In addition to
  this, permanent seminars are at work which survey such problems

as the intra-Party and internal political struggle in China, the 'Cultural Revolution', Chinese emigration in different countries, etc. The Centre issues the *Journal of Oriental Studies* in which articles on the problems of contemporary China and the Far East appear.

- *The Institute of Modern Asian Studies* at the Hong Kong University. Founded in 1963, it works in close contact with the Centre of Asian Studies. The well-known expert on the Chinese economy R. Sya is its head. The institute conducts research into various aspects of life in contemporary China and organizes seminars on the problems of China and other Asiatic countries. The Institute publishes the weekly *Mainland China Review* and *Contemporary China Economic and Social Studies*. Articles and documents are published in these reviews which throw light on the contemporary economic and political development of China together with the international relations of the PRC.
- *The Institute of Far Eastern Studies* at the Chinese University of Hong Kong. Founded in 1962, its Director Van Ho–chun is a specialist in present-day Chinese politics and was educated in England. The institute co-ordinates research carried out by different departments of the Chinese University on Far Eastern problems, works out new methods of studying China and organizes discussions and conferences.
- *The Institute of Advanced Chinese Studies and Research* at the Chinese University has been in existence since 1953. Wu Tsun–Chen is head of the Institute, which pursues reseach into the history, philosophy and literature of China.
- *The Institute of Chinese Studies* at the Chinese University. Opened in 1967, it trains students to become experts on China and carries out scientific research work on Chinese problems.
- The Centre for the collection and analysis of information on the situation within China. Created and owned by the Jesuit order. The well-known Jesuit Sinologue Ladani is its director.

Taiwan and pro-Taiwanese organizations in Hong Kong
- *The Central News Agency,* Bank of East Asia Building, 10 Des Voeux Rd; telephone H-238522.
- *The Hong Kong Trade Union Council.*

SEVEROV
[GRUSHKO]

All three of the countries where the Centre found intelligence operations most difficult to conduct – Albania, China and North Korea – were Communist states outside the Soviet bloc. Tight security in Kim Il Sung's neo-Stalinist police state made the work of the KGB Residency in Pyongyang as difficult as in Beijing. Moscow viewed with alarm Kim's growing flirtation with China during the early 1970s. In 1973 the Soviet Union suspended arms shipments, and the PRC became North Korea's main arms supplier. Two years later during what the North Korean press portrayed as a triumphal tour of foreign capitals, Kim Il Sung visited Beijing and Bucharest but missed out Moscow.

The KGB regarded Kim himself with feelings of both betrayal and contempt. Kim posed as a wartime resistance hero who had freed his country from the Japanese yoke in August 1945 after a partisan campaign of unsurpassed brilliance. The Centre, however, was well aware that Kim had not even been in Korea in August 1945. While Korea was being liberated by Soviet troops, Kim had been serving in Russia as both a lieutenant in the Red Army and an agent of the NKVD (the predecessor of the KGB).

Because of the difficulty of intelligence collection inside North Korea, most KGB operations against it were conducted in foreign capitals where Kim's regime had diplomatic missions – a strategy similar to that employed against the PRC. North Korean embassies, however, were thinner on the ground than those of China. In the West the main centre for KGB operations was Scandinavia, all four of whose capitals contained North Korean embassies. (Elsewhere in Europe, only Austria and Portugal had diplomatic relations with Pyongyang.) The most successful of the Scandinavian Residencies was that of Copenhagen, which succeeded in obtaining intelligence on North Korea via sources in both the Danish Socialist People's Party, a splinter group which had broken away from the Communist Party, and the Danish–North Korean Friendship Society, founded in the spring of 1976.[21]

The Centre was particularly pleased with a report obtained by the Copenhagen Residency on a meeting in the summer of 1976 between Kim Il Sung and a Socialist People's Party delegation. According to the Residency's account of the meeting, Kim Il Sung had claimed that North Korea's lack of great-power status gave it an advantage over both China and Soviet Union in relations with developing countries. Kim admitted, however, to grave concern at the possibility of another Korean War. He thought China and the Soviet Union were likely to come to his aid, but admitted that he was not certain that they would. Kim then set out a plan for a world-wide solidarity movement involving Western socialists and social democrats, similar to that which had opposed the United States in Vietnam, to support his plans for Korean unification.[22]

This report was highly praised by the Centre and circulated to the Politburo. So were three more telegrams on North Korea from the Copenhagen Residency during 1977. Kim's unrealistic plan to win mass support from Western socialists led the Centre to show unnecessary nervousness about the prospect of a rapprochement between North Korea and the Socialist International. This was one of a number of topics on which it instructed the Copenhagen Residency to obtain further intelligence.

No 4774/ND   Top Secret
5 December 1977   Copy No 1

COPENHAGEN

To: The Resident

During 1977 the Residency turned its attention to the elucidation of questions concerning Korea. In the main the data received from you are of interest and supplement intelligence which we have on individual aspects of the situation in the Korean peninsula, the internal situation and the foreign policy of both the Korean People's Democratic Republic and South Korea. Out of fourteen telegraphed reports received from you in the course of this year, three were submitted to the Authorities* one was utilized in the compilation of an analytical report, your report No 952 was submitted to the leadership of our department and the remainder were filed for information.

In its foreign policy, the leadership of the Korean People's Democratic Republic is paying considerable attention at the present time to developing relations with the Scandinavian countries including Denmark and striving thereby to 'erase' the consequences of the notorious narcotics scandal. Notwithstanding their heavy indebtedness to some developed capitalist countries amounting to some 1.5 billions of dollars, the North Koreans are endeavouring to maintain their industrial–economic links with the West at the previous level, and, where possible, to increase them. Thus, for example, in June–July of this year, a large party of Danish specialists visited the Korean People's Democratic Republic to pass on experience of operating of the Sunchkhon cement factory which has been constructed there with the assistance of Japan, Denmark, Austria and other capitalist countries.

The existing data, and in particular your report No 952, confirm the interest of the Korean Labour Party in developing relations with the Socialist and Social-Democratic Parties of Western Europe, in particular with those in the Scandinavian countries on whose support the North Koreans will rely this December in Tokyo at the meeting of the Social-Democratic Party leaders within the framework of the Sotsintern [Socialist International].

We are, therefore, interested in obtaining specific information on the development of relations between the Korean People's Democratic Republic and Denmark in various spheres and, in particular, information on how the Danes are reacting to North Korean feelers regarding an increase in the links. Of particular interest would be data on the hidden meaning behind the efforts of the Korean Labour [Communist] Party to activate contacts with parties belonging to the Sotsintern.

Inasmuch as there is information indicating that the ruling parties of the Scandinavian countries co-ordinate their policies with regard to the

---

* *Instantsiya*

Korean People's Democratic Republic and concert their steps towards the development of links with the Korean Labour Party, the possibility cannot be ruled out that you may receive information on the Korean People's Democratic Republic's contacts with other countries of Northern Europe and also with the USA and the People's Republic of China. We should be extremely interested to receive any such information.

The foreign-policy stand of the Korean People's Democratic Republic and of South Korea is characterized by the endeavours of these countries to achieve the maximum consolidation of their positions in this or that region to the exclusion of their rival. We would welcome information on the respective positions of North and South Korea in the countries of your region, particularly Denmark, and information on which circles support which country.

We request you, as far as possible, in preparing intelligence reports for the Centre, not to confine yourself to evaluations emanating only from Korean representatives but to supplement these with appraisals and statements from responsible representatives of your country of residence.

SEVEROV

[V. F. GRUSHKO]

[Head of Third Department FCD]

By the end of the decade the Centre's anxieties about North Korea had somewhat diminished. Pyongyang was put out by both the Sino-American rapprochement and the Chinese invasion of Vietnam in 1979. Thereafter Soviet arms supplies to North Korea resumed. The Centre agreed to a request from North Korean intelligence for a variety of intelligence equipment. While the Chinese boycotted Red Army Day in February 1980, Pyongyang celebrated once again the 'militant friendship' between Soviet and North Korean forces.[23] Intelligence on North Korea subsequently became a less urgent priority. It was not mentioned by name in either the review of foreign operations in 1982–83 or the FCD Plan of Work for 1984.[24]

The Middle East

At the end of the 1960s Egypt seemed to offer a secure base for Soviet influence in the Middle East. In addition to the more than 20,000 Soviet advisers in Egypt, the KGB had penetrated the Egyptian bureaucracy on an impressive scale. Its agents included President Gamal Abdel Nasser's intelligence chief, Sami Sharaf. There were numerous jokes within the Centre about the 'Soviet Egyptian Republic'. But after Nasser's sudden death in September 1970, the vast edifice of Soviet influence crumbled rapidly away. Within two years Sharaf had been arrested, the Soviet advisers had been sent packing and many of the agents recruited under Nasser had broken contact. Because of heavy surveillance by Egyptian security, meetings with the agents who remained usually took place outside Egypt in locations such as Cyprus and Beirut. Nasser's successor, Anwar el-Sadat, was denounced in the Centre as a traitor. His Director of Intelligence, General Ahmed Ismail, was known to be in contact with the CIA.[25]

Sadat's unilateral denunciation of the Soviet – Egyptian friendship treaty in March 1976 caused little surprise in the FCD. In November 1976 the Centre circulated a memorandum (*zapiska*) to Residencies, accurately predicting that Sadat would continue to strengthen his ties with the West, especially the United States:

	TOP SECRET
4923/52	Copy No 1
3 November 1976	To Residents
	(according to list)

ON THE SUBJECT OF EGYPTIAN POLICY TOWARDS THE USSR AND THE USA

An analysis of the available information shows that the leadership of the ARE [Arab Republic of Egypt], headed by Sadat, is continuing its policy of widening its contacts with the West, primarily with the USA.

Sadat's policy of developing all-round co-operation with the West has not so far brought any perceptible benefits to the ARE. According to well-informed Arab diplomatic circles in Cairo, there appears to be growing disappointment on the part of the Egyptians that American economic assistance has been much less than is required in order to stabilize the ARE economy. According to available information, the Americans do not intend to help Egypt in the future to the extent required by Sadat. The US deputy Minister of Finance, Parsky, considers 'that the main course of economic co-operation between the ARE and the USA lies through the increase of private American capital investment, while assistance given through government channels must only serve as of the Egyptian economy for the assimilation of the former'. American private business is, however, approaching economic co-operation with Egypt with great caution. According to an assessment by the leadership of the International Bank for Reconstruction and Development, private investors are frightened by the internal political instability and by the inability of the present ARE administration effectively to manage the economy.

At the same time Sadat is not prepared to take measures to improve relations with the Soviet Union. The Egyptian leadership is planning very shortly to reduce to a minimum the number of Soviet military and technical specialists in the ARE and to decrease the size of Egyptian missions in the USSR. The training of Egyptian military personnel in Soviet military training establishments is being interrupted and the number of Egyptian students going to the USSR is being reduced.

According to information from Egyptian business circles, the curtailment of relations with the USSR is creating dissatisfaction in a considerable section of the Egyptian bourgeoisie, particularly among the representatives of firms specializing in the production and sale of those goods whose main buyer is the Soviet Union. The State sector of Egyptian industry remains dependent on deliveries of Soviet equipment, spare parts and raw materials. According to the view of the Counsellor of the Prime Minister, Rahman, it is more advantageous for Egypt to obtain spare parts from the USSR than to switch over to home production based on the use of Western technology and equipment.

The greatest dissatisfaction with the present foreign policy exists in army circles. It is considered in these circles that with the slowing down of the process of reaching a Middle East settlement, the danger of a renewed military conflict with Israel is increasing. Notwithstanding Sadat's efforts to diversify his sources of arms, the West has not so far given Egypt any real military help. The US Ford administration considers it expedient to start deliveries to the ARE of certain types of military equipment, but cannot overcome the resistance of the pro-Israel lobby in Congress. At the same time the cessation of deliveries of Soviet military equipment and the recall of Soviet military specialists has a bad effect on the battle-readiness of the ARE army. According to information from Egyptian military circles, more than half of their aviation equipment and a large part of their rocket, armoured and other equipment requires overhaul or replacement. According to the assessment of the American Special Services, if the United States is unable in some way to fill the vacuum which has been caused by the end of Soviet–Egyptian military co-operation, then the situation in the Egyptian army will become explosive, and the 'Army generals could decide to mount a coup'. ...*

In an effort to lessen the dissatisfaction in the country with its biased policy towards the West, the Egyptian leadership is taking certain steps, which are intended to give the impression that it is interested in the normalization of relations with the Soviet Union. Egyptian officials make statements about the ARE's desire 'to build bridges with the USSR'. This theme features in a number of Sadat's latest speeches, and the same was said by Foreign Minister Fahmi in a conversation with a Soviet representative. The President of the National Assembly, Mare, has spoken about the possibility of arranging a visit by him to the USSR by him unofficially but with Sadat's knowledge. The tone of anti-Soviet propaganda has been somewhat softened, and Egyptian representatives abroad have been instructed by the Egyptian Foreign Office to abstain from anti-Soviet actions. However, in the words of the former ARE Prime Minister, Sidki, 'the readiness of SADAT to seek a reconciliation with the USSR is a mere manoeuvre, based on expediency'.

Sadat is convinced as before that merely by showing outward signs of friendship he will be able to succeed in obtaining military-economic help from the USSR without damaging American–Egyptian relations. The ARE Ambassador in the FRG emphasized in a private conversation that 'in conducting his policy, Sadat proceeds on the basis that the strategic interests of the USSR in the Middle East will in the long run force the Soviet side to agree with the conditions laid down by Egypt'.

---

* Passage omitted.

Judging from reports received, the Egyptian government will continue to pursue the all-round development of American–Egyptian relations.

SVITOV

Despite Soviet anger at Sadat's 'betrayal', the oil crisis which followed the Arab–Israeli Yom Kippur War in 1973 encouraged the Centre's hopes for a revival of Soviet influence in the Middle East. Arab oil producers first cut off oil exports to the West, then joined other OPEC countries in enforcing an enormous rise in oil prices. For the first time, a part of the Third World had successfully brought economic pressure on the West. Moscow was taken aback by the role played by the region's leading oil producer, Saudi Arabia, which it had previously regarded as under the thumb of the United States. The Centre nurtured illusory hopes of weakening the American ties of the oil-rich Shah of Iran. (It was slow to foresee his overthrow in 1978.) The FCD also persuaded itself that political instability in Turkey might bring to power a left-wing government.

At the annual FCD Party Conference on 26 November 1975, General Kryuchkov announced that Iran and Turkey had been designated priority targets, second in importance only to the USA, NATO and the PRC. Heavy security in both countries, however, made intelligence operations 'extremely difficult'. When the later defector Vladimir Kuzichkin joined Directorate S (illegals) in 1976,[26] he discovered that there was not a single illegal working in Turkey.[27] The KGB's most important agent in Iran, the 56-year-old General Ahmed Mogharabi, recruited 30 years before, was arrested in September 1977 and later executed. There followed what Kuzichkin, then stationed in Teheran, considered 'an intelligence vacuum' in the Residency.[28] The other major state in the Middle East where operating conditions were most difficult was Saudi Arabia. Because of the absence of Soviet–Saudi diplomatic relations, the KGB lacked a legal Residency in Riyadh.

The head of Directorate S, Vladimir Kirpichenko, a Middle Eastern expert whose past successes included the recruitment of

Sami Sharaf, won Kryuchkov's support for a plan to recruit Iranian, Turkish and Saudi students and expatriates in Europe as illegal agents for use in their home countries.

Outgoing No 20302/N   Top Secret
30 December 1977   Copy No 1
To Residents
(According to distribution list)

On account of the extremely complicated agent-operational conditions in Iran, Turkey and Saudi Arabia which make the conduct of intelligence work particularly difficult in these countries, and in accordance with forward plans approved by Comrade Sviridov [Andropov], it is intended in the near future to mount a complex of measures to step up work in the above-mentioned countries on an illegal basis. To this end, and in conjunction with the resources of the Centre and of legal Residencies in countries of the Near and Middle East, it is envisaged that the active use of the resources of a number of Residencies in European countries will also be required.

In view of the fact that a relatively large number of young students and expatriates from Iran, Turkey and Saudi Arabia are in Europe at the present time it is essential to start work on selecting from among this category of person candidates whose services we may be able to utilize for Line N purposes in the very near future.

In the light of the directives of Comrade Alyoshin [Kryuchkov], No 3994/N of 28.3.75 and No 7059 of 17.6.76 with which you are familiar, we request you to outline ways and means of stepping up the work of selection, study and deep study of candidates for subsequent use for illegal intelligence purposes in the above mentioned countries. This will mean:

- a thorough analysis of the agent resources and other assets of the Residency to identify persons who may be of use in the plan already mentioned; in this connection it is also desirable to analyse available material on agents and confidential contacts who have lost their potential in Europe;

- the organization of work in order to select and study candidates from among Iranian, Turkish and Saudi Arabian citizens who possess real possibilities for carrying out intelligence work as special [illegal] agents or as agent-employers;

- the identification of candidates from among the citizens of other countries of the Near and Middle East who have opportunities to travel to Iran, Turkey or Saudi Arabia for extended periods;
- bearing in mind the large number of technical specialists who travel from the European countries to take up employment in Iran, Turkey and Saudi Arabia, a purposeful effort should be undertaken to make a deep study of candidates from this category of persons with a view to their subsequent despatch to the countries already mentioned.

Suggestions on the foregoing to reach this office by 1 March 1978.

VADIMOV
[KIRPICHENKO]
[Head of Directorate S, FCD]

Though the Centre did not foresee the Islamic Revolution which brought the Ayatollah Khomeini to power in Iran in early 1979, it was cautiously optimistic about its consequences, hoping that the Marxist Tudeh party and other left-wing groups would be able to play an influential role in the new regime. Social change, it believed, would make Iran more progressive and better disposed to the Soviet Union.

In May 1979 the high-flying Leonid Vladimirovich Shebarshin (later to succeed Kryuchkov as head of the FCD) was posted as Resident in Teheran with personal instructions from Andropov to rebuild an Iranian agent network within two years. He did not succeed. In 1980 13 Soviet intelligence officers and diplomats were ordered to leave. A year later, the two leading KGB illegals in Iran were arrested in Switzerland.[29] At the end of 1981 KGB Residencies in Teheran and elsewhere were instructed to draw up four-year plans for increasing Soviet influence in Iran. The plans proved hopelessly optimistic. In 1982, while serving as a Line N officer in Teheran, Kuzichkin defected to SIS. In 1983 the Tudeh Party was dissolved; 18 Soviet intelligence officers (including Shebarshin), diplomats and their families were expelled.

During the later 1970s Moscow's closest major ally in the Middle East was Saddam Hussein's Iraq. In 1977 the Centre informed Residencies that, by decision of the Party Central

Committee, in view of the close relations established between Iraq and the Soviet Union, all intelligence operations against Iraq were to cease forthwith. Existing Iraqi agents and 'confidential contacts' were to be downgraded to 'official contacts'. No other state outside the Soviet bloc benefited from such a self-denying ordinance on the part of the Soviet intelligence community. When Saddam Hussein began imprisoning large numbers of Iraqi Communists in April 1979, the ordinance was lifted.

Soviet–Iraqi relations were further complicated when Saddam began the Gulf War with Iran in September 1980. Moscow eventually decided to give secret backing to Iraq but remained deeply suspicious of Saddam himself.[30] Shortly before Gordievsky's recall to Moscow in May 1985, the London Residency received an urgent request for all possible intelligence on Iraqi preparations for chemical and biological warfare and on assistance for these preparations from abroad.[31]

Zionism and Israel

'Zionist subversion' was one of the KGB's most enduring conspiracy theories. The Stalinist era bequeathed to the KGB a tradition of antisemitism masquerading as anti-Zionism still clearly visible even in the mid-1980s. In 1948, however, the Soviet Union had been the first to recognize the state of Israel, seeing its creation as a blow to British imperialism inflicted by progressive Jews of Russian and Polish origin. Alarm at the enthusiasm shown by Soviet Jews for the new state, combined with evidence of Israel's growing links with the United States, produced a rapid *volte-face* in Soviet policy. Henceforth, Zionism was officially condemned as part of an imperialist plot to subvert the Soviet Union.

The campaign against imaginary Zionist conspirators spread throughout the Soviet bloc. The 1952 trial of the 'Leadership of the Anti-State Conspiratorial Centre led by Rudolf Slánský' in Czechoslovakia identified 11 of the 14 defendants, including Slánský himself, as 'of Jewish origin'. The simultaneous purge of Jews from the Soviet nomenklatura was nowhere more energetically pursued than at the Centre. By early 1953 all Jews had been removed from the MGB (predecessor of the KGB), save for a small number of 'hidden Jews': people of partly Jewish origin who were registered as members of other ethnic groups. In the winter of 1952–53 the MGB crushed a non-existent 'Jewish doctors' plot' against Stalin and the Soviet leadership, unmasking a group of innocent doctors as 'monsters and murderers' working for a 'corrupt Jewish bourgeois nationalist organization' in the service of Anglo-American intelligence.[32]

Though the level of anti-Zionist and antisemitic paranoia dropped sharply after Stalin's death in March 1953, it did not disappear. None of the Jews sacked from the MGB at the height of the antisemitic witch-hunt was reinstated. Over 40 years later, at the beginning of the Gorbachev era, Jews were still excluded (along with a number of other national minorities) from the KGB. The only exceptions were a handful of recruits with Jewish mothers and non-Jewish fathers, registered as members of other ethnic groups. Even the Central Committee of the Communist Party was slightly less rigid than the KGB in rejecting applicants with Jewish blood.

In the mid-1980s bizarre conspiracy theories about Jewish and Zionist plots continued to surface at the Centre. L.P. Zamoysky, deputy head of the FCD Directorate of Intelligence Information, an officer with a reputation for high intelligence and good judgement, solemnly assured the London KGB Residency in January 1985, in Gordievsky's presence, that Zionism had behind it not merely Jewish big business and finance but also the occult power of Freemasonry whose rites, he alleged, were of Jewish origin. It was, he insisted, a 'fact' that Freemasons were an integral part of the Zionist conspiracy. Many KGB officers believed that the US 'military-industrial complex', which they saw as the Soviet bloc's most dangerous opponent, was manipulated by the 'Jewish lobby'. The Fifth Directorate of the KGB, founded in 1968 to monitor and suppress domestic dissidence in all its forms, regarded Zionism as the main channel for Western 'ideological subversion' in the Soviet Union.[33]

In 1968–69 Soviet Jews began a letter-writing campaign to Western journalists and the samizdat press, protesting at the violation of their human rights. After a mass Jewish sit-in at the Supreme Soviet building early in 1971, there was a dramatic increase in the number of exit visas granted for emigration to Israel. The Politburo's decision seems to have been intended both as a concession to Western opinion at a time when it was pursuing East–West détente, and as a means of pacifying dissidents who, it may have calculated, would not jeopardize their prospects of emigration by continued agitation. Over a quarter of a million Jews were allowed to emigrate during the 1970s before détente gave way to renewed confrontation with the United States. Yuri Andropov, the KGB Chairman, is believed to have concluded that the emigration policy had failed. It had not produced the trade and credit concessions which, it was claimed, the United States had promised as a quid pro quo. Nor had it pacified the Jewish 'refuseniks', who were supported by a vociferous campaign of international protest. In 1978 one of the best-known refuseniks, Anatoli Shcharansky, was sentenced to ten years in a labour camp, plus three further years' imprisonment, on a trumped-up charge of 'treasonable' links with the CIA.[34]

By the beginning of the 1980s the KGB, and in particular its Fifth Directorate, was concerned by other nationality problems as well as the Jewish refuseniks: among them Tartars deported by Stalin who wanted to return; Baltic nationalists who were demanding greater independence; and Armenians and Volga Germans who wanted to emigrate. The Centre also feared that the surge of Islamic fundamentalism in the Middle East might spread across Soviet borders. The FCD conference held to review foreign operations during 1982–83 was told of 'a marked increase' in 'the subversive activity of émigré, nationalist and Zionist organizations and associations abroad'. Zionism, however, still retained pride of place among the subversive forces which the Centre believed were in league with Western intelligence agencies. The FCD 'Plan of Work' for 1984 listed first in its counter-intelligence priority targets:

> Plans for subversion action or secret operations by the adversary's special services, and by centre for ideological diversion and nationalists, especially Zionists and other anti-Soviet organizations, against the USSR and other countries of the socialist community.[35]

In the summer of 1982 Residents were sent a detailed four-year 'Plan for Work against Zionism in 1982–1986', which had been under preparation for some time.[36] The Centre warned that the Soviet bloc was threatened by 'all kinds of subversive operations' organized by Zionists in league with Israel and Western intelligence services. These had to be countered by a major increase in intelligence collection and agent recruitment, as well as by a wide range of active measures designed to weaken and divide the Zionist movement.

No 1214/PR   TOP SECRET
02.07.82   Copy No. 1
                        To: Residents
                    according to the list

We are sending you an extract from the prospective plan for work
against Zionism in 1982–1986, for your information and for use in
your work.

Information and analysis, influence operations and recruitment and
agent-operational measures in this line must be included in the prescribed form in Residencies' annual plans and reports.

Attachment. Extract No 471/PR/54 Top Secret, Copy No 1 of 9 pages,
PN.

                            SILIN
                          [G F TITOV]
              [Head of the Third Department, FCD]

Attachment to No 1214/PR   Top Secret
No 471/PR/54   Copy No 1
02.07.82

EXTRACT FROM THE PROSPECTIVE PLAN OF WORK AGAINST ZIONISM
IN 1982–86

I. Work on information and analysis

1. Step up information-gathering on the following questions through
KGB foreign intelligence channels:

– plans, forms and methods of international Zionist subversion (The
  World Zionist Organization (WZO), the 'Jewish Agency', the
  World Jewish Congress, (WJC), the Zionist Israeli Leadership, the
  Israeli special services and also the numerous Zionist organizations
  active throughout the world, chiefly in the principal capitalist
  countries); co-operation between the Israeli special services and
  international Zionist centres and imperialist intelligence services,
  and in the first place, the Central Intelligence Agency of the USA.

- preparation by the Israeli special services and Zionist centres (possibly in contact with the intelligence services of the leading capitalist states), of specific ideological sabotage and all kinds of subversive operations against the USSR, other countries of the socialist community and the international communist and workers' movement;
- alignment of forces in international Zionism: the relative importance of the leftist-liberal wing, which, in contrast to the rightist-extremist wing, advocates the establishment of normal mutual relations between West and East;
- disagreements in the Zionist leadership over organizing and conducting subversion; the attitude of individual leaders of international Zionism to the question of Jewish emigration to Israel, especially from the USSR, and to the problem of settling Near East affairs; possible clashes in the Zionist leadership over the careerist ambitions of certain prominent Zionist figures, struggle between American and Israeli Zionists for the leading role in the Zionist movement, and conflicts between them due to the tension developing from time to time in American–Israeli relations;
- mutual relations between Zionist centres and organizations and the government of the countries where they are located, Zionist lobbies in the government and parliaments of these countries and the degree of influence they exercise on their domestic and foreign policy; conflict between the policy of Israel and the Zionist centres and the interests of Jewish business circles in the principal capitalist countries, and in particular, individual aspects of Israeli policy in the Near East, which do not suit the United States' military-industrial complex and the representatives of Israeli big business connected with it;
- any persons of Jewish origin who hold anti-Zionist views in governmental, parliamentary or political circles, in the mass media, in the business world or in the scientific or technical fields in the principal capitalist countries; information about representatives of Jewish business circles who are in favour of developing commercial and economic relations and scientific and technical co-operation with the USSR;
- political trends in Jewish communities abroad; are there any strata or individuals in them holding views close to ours on this or that subject?
- development of anti-Zionist processes and tendencies in Jewish

communities and appearance of new anti-Zionist organisations (of the type of the 'Breir' organization founded in 1972 to unite prominent figures of Jewish communities in the USA against Israeli righ-wing extremist policy and, in particular, putting forward a programme for settlement in the Near East corresponding largely to our own position on this matter);
– the attitude and mood among Jews who left the USSR after 1967 and, where possible, factual information about the number of persons desirous of returning to the USSR; possible attempts on their part to form organizations and societies for contacts with the homeland, and efforts to establish contacts with progressive Russian organizations.

Time limit: throughout the period

II. Active Measures

Work on active measures must be conducted on the following principal lines:

1. Bringing disorganization and division into the Zionist leadership by intensifying existing disagreements and conflicts:

a) between the Zionist government of Israel and the WJC leaders who, like Israel, lay claim to the role of unique representative of the so-called 'world-wide Jewish community';
b) between the liberal wing of the WJC and right-wing extremist forces in international Zionism (the WZO, the Israeli government) regarding methods of carrying on subversion against the USSR and other socialist countries and the question of Jewish immigration to Israel;
c) between Israeli and American Zionists for the leading position in the Zionist 'movement';
d) between Israeli Zionists and certain Zionist circles in the USA, whose slogan is 'independence of the Diaspora from Israel';
e) between Israeli and the United States which is obliged to manoeuvre in its relations with Israel because of its dependence on oil-producing Arab countries;
f) between the Reagan administration and the WJC, which is opposed to the present US administration, etc.

2. Freezing the initiative of the reactionary rightist–extremist wing of international Zionism by:

a) wide-ranging exposure of Zionism as a close associate of the most reactionary imperialist circles operating against peace-loving forces;

b) running operational ploys with leaders of the World Jewish Congress utilizing their fears that intensification of the 'cold' war may lead to isolation of the WJC from Jewish populations in the socialist countries;

c) disruption of Zionist-sponsored congresses and other anti-Soviet gatherings and also various kinds of ideological sabotage and various other subversive operations;

3. Weakening the influence of international Zionism, promoting the development of positive anti-Zionist tendencies and processes in Jewish communities overseas and stepping up the activity of progressive forces within them by:

a) conveying to broad strata of the Jewish population in capitalist countries information showing that the political policy of Zionist centres is directed towards undermining détente and worsening relations between East and West, and is against their vital interests;

b) compromising the most active Zionist leaders who are the initiators of various kinds of anti-Soviet operations in the international arena;

c) exposing the falsity and bankruptcy of Zionist ideology, which is serving the mercenary interest of the Jewish grande bourgeoisie;

d) disseminating information to refute the slanderous inventions of Zionists about state antisemitism allegedly existing in the USSR;

e) exerting purposeful influence through existing agent facilities and confidential contacts, especially agents of influence (not only among persons of Jewish extraction) on neutral vacillating, left-wing liberal and also former progressive groups of the Jewish population to reorientate them politically and weaken the influence of Zionism on them;

f) establishing contacts through Soviet institutions abroad, for utilization in our interests, with prominent figures in Jewish circles overseas who are in favour of developing political relations and economic or scientific, technological and cultural co-operation with the USSR; introducing the practice of inviting them to receptions at Soviet institutions abroad, helping them in suitable cases to arrange trips to the Soviet Union and to publish objective material in the Western press about the position of Jews in the USSR;

g) making open or 'covert' use of leaders of Jewish organizations who for one reason or another are against Zionism, *inter alia* by approaching them through progressive (émigré or local) Jewish organization or groups, including:

- pacifist Jewish organizations, condemning the aggressive political line of the right-wing extremist leadership and the present Israeli government aimed at disrupting détente and whipping up international tension;
- left-wing liberal Jewish organizations, comprising realistically thinking representatives of the Jewish intelligentsia and lower and middle business circles and also the rabbis who favour a just settlement in the Near East, maintaining the inalienable rights of the Arab people of Palestine;
- Jewish religious organizations representing Orthodox Judaism (not acknowledging the Jewish state of Israel, set up in violation of Judaic religious dogma and infringing by its actions a number of Talmudic canons);
- Jewish organizations rejecting the Zionist concept of a 'world-wide Jewish nation' with its centre in Israel and also the idea of emigration of all Jews to Israel, etc; also persons who are associated with publication of newspapers or other periodicals (including non-Jewish ones) promoting anti-Zionist ideas of one kind or another.

Time limit – throughout the period

h) encouraging various groups of Jews who are forbidden to return to the USSR to form compatriot organizations and societies for cultural relations with, the homeland, providing them with moral support through the Rodina [homeland] Society, and help with suitable propaganda material, converting them by this means into centres of anti-Zionism overseas.

Persons who come forward on their own initiative in favour of uniting Jews who came from the USSR in progressive organizations must be carefully checked and proposals suggested for working with them;

i) fostering the existing attraction which some Jews who were formerly in the USSR feel towards Russian progressive organizations abroad, where such tendencies can be exploited to discredit Zionism.

Prepare proposals for specific action on this point:

j) facilitating the return to the homeland of some Jews who have left the USSR and making use of them for anti-Zionist propaganda measures; co-opting for involvement in such operations 'blown' agents, those who have lost their access or some who have been specially trained for this purpose;

Time limit – December 1982

h) implementing measures designed to step up the activity of progressive organizations and also of the surviving sound stratum in formerly left-wing organizations whose leaders after the 1967 Arab–Israeli conflict in the main went over to the Zionist camp; strengthening and improving the soundness of such organizations by replenishing them with people originally from the USSR who hold anti-Zionist views, penetrating them with our agents or confidential informants who are able by their personal qualities and organizing capacity to activate the resources mentioned and involve them in anti-Zionist activity. If an opportunity is found for carrying out such an operation, please put forward proposals.

Time limit – throughout the period

III. Agent-operational support

In order to deal with the tasks mentioned above in the area of our work on information and analysis and on active measures, steps must be taken to make more effective use of the existing agent access to Zionism and create fresh access.

1. a) Step up penetration by agents and technical operations into our main targets in Zionism:

- the World Zionist Organization – WZO (General council, executive committee and its 12 departments);
- the 'Jewish Agency' (management council, executive committee);
- the World Jewish Congress – WJC (general council management council, executive committee and WJC branches in 69 countries);
- the Israeli state apparatus (the President's Office Council of Ministers, Foreign Ministry, the Ministry for Absorption, the Israeli special services – Mossad, Shinbet, Sherut-medein);

b) Acquiring fresh access and widening existing access to the Jewish press and other periodicals in order to make use of them for active measures against Zionism.

Time limit – throughout the period

2. In view of international Zionism's efforts to draw moderate Jewish groups into its sphere of influence, steps must be taken to organize

work and acquire agents in that stratum of Jewish communities with a view to subsequently moving them into Zionist centres.

3. Recruitment work must be carried out among Jews who have gone abroad and who as a result of disenchantment with life in the West feel an inclination to re-emigrate, but who for a number of reasons (including fears of revenge on the part of Zionist terrorist organizations) do not apply to Soviet consulate and conceal their views from those around them. Organize a search for and cultivation of such persons in residencies of countries where there is a Jewish colony of people who emigrated from the USSR after 1967.

Time limit – throughout the period

4. In view of the fact that some persons of Jewish origin with ethnic connections with the USSR, who live in capitalist countries, are in many cases by virtue of their position and type of occupation in possession of intelligence information (on politics, science and technology or military strategy), the search for and recruitment of such agents should not be confined to work against Zionism, and attention should be directed also to acquiring agents who have access to any secret information of interest to the USSR, and who present opportunities for carrying out large-scale influence operations. The work of recruitment must be stepped up among persons of Jewish origin who visit the USSR as part of various types of delegation.

Time limit – throughout the period

5. When carrying out subsidiary tasks in our work against Zionism (keeping a check on the activity of the Zionist lobby in capitalist countries, obtaining leads, studying candidates for recruitment etc) wide use must be made of agents of non-Jewish origin who because of their type of activity have constant contact with this or that group of the Jewish population in the country.

Time limit – throughout the period

Ciphers and Counter-Intelligence

All Soviet missions in the West can expect surveillance by local security services. The Centre, however, had an apparently incurable tendency to exaggerate both its scale and intensity. Before leaving for foreign postings, all KGB officers went through a training course designed to prepare them for all manner of 'provocations' by Western intelligence agencies. The training, however, was based on a frequently false analogy with the huge KGB surveillance operations conducted within the Soviet Union.

In Gordievsky's experience at London and Copenhagen, new arrivals began by suspecting even local shopkeepers and gardeners in nearby parks of being part of an elaborate network designed to keep them under constant surveillance. Most eventually grasped the fact that Western security services are tiny by Soviet standards and have to choose their targets far more selectively than the KGB. Directorate K at the Centre, however, continued to issue sometimes fanciful warnings about new forms of surveillance being devised in the West, and to interpret misfortunes suffered by Soviet citizens abroad as possible – or probable – provocations by local security services.

Among those who the Centre feared were the main targets for Western provocation were Soviet cipher personnel. The Centre's fears were largely a reflection of its own successes in this field. Most major codebreaking successes on which evidence is available have been assisted in varying degrees by intelligence on foreign code and cipher systems obtained by espionage. Western intelligence agencies, however, did not make such intelligence a major priority until the Second World War. Russia already did so at the beginning of the century. The British ambassador to St. Petersburg, Sir Charles Hardinge, complained in 1906 that the Tsarist Okhrana had offered his head Chancery servant the then enormous sum of £1,000 to steal one of the British diplomatic ciphers.[37] Between the wars Soviet intelligence revived and expanded Tsarist techniques for obtaining Western cipher materials and diplomatic documents to assist its codebreakers. Its first major success in penetrating Whitehall was to recruit two Foreign Office code clerks, Ernest Oldham in 1930 and John King in 1935.[38]

A generation later, the passing of the age of the brilliantly talented ideological mole in both Britain and the United States increased still further the relative importance of agents such as Oldham and King. The vast Anglo-American communications and sigint (signals intelligence) network contained thousands of comparatively junior employees with access to high-grade intelligence. By the 1970s the KGB's most important moles in the United States and Britain were no longer high fliers like Kim Philby and Alger Hiss, but two cunning though not especially talented petty criminals. Chief Warrant Officer John Walker, a communications watch officer on the staff of the Commander of US Submarine Forces in the Atlantic, had joined the navy as a teenage high school dropout in order to escape imprisonment after committing four serious burglaries, and later tried to force his wife into prostitution. Corporal Geoffrey Prime of the Royal Air Force and, later, the British sigint agency GCHQ was a social and sexual misfit who graduated from making obscene telephone calls to molesting little girls. Both Walker and Prime occupied comparatively low-level jobs which gave them – and the KGB – access to some of the most important cipher and sigint secrets of the Atlantic Alliance.

The almost simultaneous recruitment of Walker and Prime in January 1968 helped to prompt a major reorganization of KGB sigint. Hitherto the Eighth Directorate had handled sigint as well as KGB ciphers and communications security. In 1969 a new Sixteenth Directorate was established to specialize exclusively in sigint. The new directorate worked closely with the Sixteenth Department of the First Chief Directorate which henceforth had exclusive control of all FCD operations to acquire foreign code and cipher systems, and to penetrate sigint agencies. Its officers in Residencies abroad handled only one case each which they kept entirely separate from other Residency operations.[39]

The Centre was haunted by the fear that Western intelligence agencies might discover Walkers and Primes within the Soviet cipher and sigint organization. These fears were sometimes taken to remarkable lengths. Even dry cleaning shops, Directorate K believed, might be used to target Soviet cipher clerks. In March 1985 the Centre began two elaborate operations, codenamed Blesna 6 and Blesna 7, designed to detect this and other, mostly improbable, Western traps.

Comr YAN
[Ms.:]
Lavrov, 21 March 85

No 161
Top Secret
Copy No 1
LONDON
To Comrade LAVROV [NIKITENKO]
(personal)

No 312/KR
13 March 1985

IMPLEMENTATION OF MEASURES 'BLESNA-6 AND 7'

In compliance with the instructions from the heads of our Department for stepping up security in Soviet institutions and their secret cipher offices abroad, the Centre has been studying the question of applying special measures (codename 'Blesna-6 and 7') with the aim of uncovering any possible attempts by the adversary's special services to introduce devices and markers into the personal effects of cipher staff while local consumer services firms have access to these articles.

Application of the measures will, in addition, be designed to obtain specimens of new equipment used by the adversary's technical intelligence services to obtain information processed in UZTS* in Soviet missions abroad.

'Blesna-6' envisages setting up a suitable situation for the enemy to step up operations for technical processing of personal articles belonging to one of our cipher clerks, which have been given in for repair, dry cleaning or other services.

---

* secure cipher rooms

'Blesna-7' is applied when a cipher clerk purchases some personal article in local shops or from a commercial firm, after previously selecting or ordering it, so that the article remains outside our control for a certain length of time.

Ways of arousing the interest of the adversary's special services will be devised by the Residency with reference to the operational situation in the country and local customs. At the same time, it is essential in the first place to concentrate on commercial firms, stores, studios, cleaners etc, where the adversary would (or could) carry out operations against Soviet nationals, and to analyse any incidents involving members of the Soviet community which may have taken place there.

It is also evident that a single visit to a selected objective will scarcely lead to the desired result. When planning these measures, therefore, one must envisage several calls, having regard to the usual pattern of visits by Soviet nationals to these places and the availability of goods on the local market.

In order to carry out these measures it is considered advisable that an operational team should be formed, consisting of a cipher clerk, or an engineer (if there is one) for the security of the UZTS, and a member of the Residency who speaks the local language. In our view one should involve in this operation any operational personnel who have been to some extent 'blown' to the adversary and whose repeated visits to the 'consumer establishment' must therefore come within the range of vision of the adversary's special services. We also assume that, from knowledge of the functional duties and general behaviour of Referentura [Cipher section] officials, the adversary is able to distinguish a cipher clerk from other Soviet nationals visiting shops or consumer services. Cipher clerks could be used at the time when it is planned to replace them and this will enable us to provide a cover story for our operation, resulting from the need to purchase articles for personal use.

The following articles could be used for operations 'Blesna-6 and 7':

- shoes with heels
- electronic wristwatch with alarm
- jacket (suit)
- fountain pen (with a built-in electronic watch)
- lighter
- wallet and notebook (with hard covers) etc

The decision about the form of delivery of the goods (whether by those carrying out the operation or through a firm) will be taken locally. The expenses of the operation will be put down to the Centre's account.

All articles obtained in the course of the operation or processed by consumer services must be despatched to the Centre for expert examination (this is not done locally).

Please assess your facilities, in the light of the above, for carrying out operations 'Blesna-6 and 7', examine the variants for mounting the operation, designate candidates for carrying it out, for submission to the corresponding subsections in the Centre for approval, and also inform us of the proposed expenditure.

Please exercise personal control over preparation for these set tasks; and inform only your 'KR' deputy of the nature of the assignment.

Please send your proposals by diplomatic bag addressed to Comrade Krylov and marked 'Personal'.

VLADIMIROV

[A.T. KIREEV]

[Head of Directorate K, FCD]

Each Soviet diplomatic mission abroad had a secure cipher section known as the Referentura divided into separate departments handling diplomatic, KGB, GRU and other communications. Life for Referentura staff was more strictly regulated than for any other Soviet officials living abroad. When moving about the capitals in which they were stationed they had at all times to be accompanied by embassy staff. Unsurprisingly, alcoholism within Referenturas was a recurrent problem. A study by the Centre early in 1985 revealed that this and other problems were worst among those cipher staff who had spent most time abroad. General Kryuchkov, himself teetotal, was so concerned by the security risks involved that in March 1985 he sent personal directives to all Residents to insist on 'standards and rules of conduct by cipher service personnel'.

No 5482/PR   No 201
23.3.1985   Secret
                                                              Copy No 1
              To residents and KGB representatives
                     (according to list)
                         Personal

WORK WITH EMPLOYEES OF SECRET CIPHER SERVICES ABROAD

Cases of breaches of rules and regulations for conduct abroad on the
part of members of secret cipher services have recently become more
frequent and in 1984 alone made it necessary to send 12 employees in
this category home to the Soviet Union before their time.

Analysis of the reasons for these dismissals has shown that as a rule
the basic cause is misconduct due to abuse of alcohol, abnormal family
relations, lack of discipline and slackness at work, and that it is most
frequent of all among employees who have had three or more postings
abroad.

For instance, in March 1984, a senior Referentura Officer at the
USSR's commercial mission in Mexico was sent home early from his
posting abroad because during his period of residence in the country
(since March 1983) he had consistently indulged in alcohol abuse,
which was the reason for the unhappy situation in his family. In spite of
educational work done with him, he did not draw the necessary
conclusions for himself, but continued to drink heavily. Late in 1983 he
went home during working hours, drank himself into a condition in
which he was no longer responsible, and in consequence, was in-
capable of carrying out his duties.

In August 1984 a Referentura officer of the Soviet MFA was sent
home early from Cameroon as a result of an abnormal family situation.
His wife accused him of conjugal infidelity and declared her intention
of dissolving the marriage, which gave rise to a serious scandal in the
family, and on this account it proved impossible for the couple to
remain abroad.

It is a disturbing fact that those who commit serious offences in
Soviet communities are often the heads of Referenturas, i.e. the very
persons who have to exercise control to see that cipher service officers
observe the rules of conduct abroad, look after their training and be an
example of behaviour for their subordinates.

Another instance occurred in August 1984, when the head of the

Referentura at the Soviet Embassy in Mali committed suicide at night in his flat with a pistol taken from the Referentura.

Before this incident, he had several times indulged in alcohol abuse and been found in a state of intoxication and he was not always in control of his actions. For several days before his suicide, he had stayed away from his duties and in view of this it was decided that he should be sent home early.

In October 1984, the acting head of the Referentura at the Soviet mission in Kampuchea was sent home early to the USSR for systematic alcohol abuse and for striking a courier from the special protection service in the face.

This sort of situation is evidence of the fact that less attention is being given to this category of employee of Soviet establishments by those in charge of Soviet missions abroad, residences and especially security officers, and inadequate educational work is being done for them.

In view of this we think the following action must be taken:

- improve the standard of counter-intelligence work in the Referentura of missions abroad. Endeavour, jointly with the heads of Soviet establishments and Party officials, to step up educational work among employees of the cipher service and pay more attention to the way of life and leisure occupations of this category of personnel. Be well aware of relations within their families. Exercise a positive influence on the situation among Referentura staff;
- see that there is a prompt reaction to any circumstances providing evidence of infringement of rules of conduct abroad on the part of members of the cipher service, or of alcohol abuse;
- step up checks on observance by cipher service personnel of the arrangements laid down for going into town, to see that they fulfil the requirement that they should be constantly (inseparably) accompanied by Embassy officials on visits to town.

At the same time, having regard to the specific character of this category of employee, such action should be undertaken with great care, endeavouring to involve the administration and Party organizations in it to a greater extent. There must be strict regard for secrecy in any operational measures undertaken.

The Centre must be informed immediately of any incident of infringement of standards and rules of conduct by cipher service personnel.

ALYOSHIN

[KRYUCHKOV]

The Centre was also continually fearful that its agent network included 'plants' by Western intelligence services. It insisted on enormously detailed and time-consuming checks on the reliability of both actual and prospective agents:

gzh-1   Top Secret
No 6631/X   Copy No 1
24 May 1978

COPENHAGEN
To: Comrade KORIN [LYUBIMOV]

We are forwarding herewith a report entitled 'Basic methods for conducting checks on agents, and deep study targets among foreigners abroad', which has been prepared by the appropriate sub-section of our service for possible use when planning checking measures on the existing agent network, future targets of deep study and operational contacts.
Attachment on 16 pages, Secret No 151/2–6650 DM.
[Ms note]
Please inform all members of the operational staff. This material must be used when drafting the relevant proposals.
                        KORIN [LYUBIMOV]
                              6.6.78

                                                        SECRET
                                                      Copy No 1
                                            Attachment to No 6631/X

BASIC METHODS FOR CHECKING AGENTS AND DEEP STUDY TARGETS AMONG FOREIGNERS ABROAD

The following are the basic and essential requirements by which Residencies must be guided in their daily operational practice in order to guarantee security in their work with foreign agents:

1. The checking of an agent apparatus must be a continuous process,

irrespective of the basis on which the agent was recruited, the degree of confidence we have in him or the length of time he has been collaborating with us;

2. Well thought-out agent checks must be carried out *not more than once a year* and, should any doubts regarding reliability crop up, a complex of special checks using operational-technical methods must be implemented;

3. The above-mentioned checks must pursue strictly defined aims, conform to the specific circumstances and realistic possibilities, as well as being based on the results of an analysis of all available material and an assessment of previous work with the agent.

The basic aim of these checks must be the acquisition of reliable data enabling conclusions to be drawn concerning the following problems:

- whether the person being checked has links with hostile special services and is acting on their behalf (check for plants);
- whether the person being checked is a deep study target for hostile Special Services (check for loss of cover);
- whether he is sincerely co-operating with us and making active use of his intelligence potential (check on sincerity);

In practical operational work the methods listed below for studying and carrying out checks on agents may be used.

I. Methods of conducting checks without the use of agents

1. *The studying and checking of an agent in the course of personal contact between him and a case officer.*

- By accumulating biographical and character data on the agent and by rechecking this periodically;
- By regularly highlighting any changes in the agent's political or ideological views as well as changes in his work – or social circumstances; a realistic appraisal of the reasons for his collaborating with us and his intelligence potential;
- By determining his reactions to tasks of an operational and test nature, to discussions on his personal life, his sources of information etc;
- By collecting data on the agent's close contacts and the subsequent checking of these through existing means;
- Any changes in the agent's family circumstances, inter-relationships within the family; his lifestyle;

- By his observance of security measures in performing intelligence tasks, the clandestinity of his behaviour;
- By periodical checks as to how the agent is observing the conditions for contacting and cover-stories concerning his intelligence activity.

2. The checking of an agent through official means
Various kinds of official sources of information comprising institutional and biographical information on governmental, political and commercial personalities may be used:

- telephone directories;
- parliamentary, party and company directories;
- newspapers and journals;
- official archives and libraries;
- Police Department bulletins;
- the facilities offered by Chambers of Commerce, banks, companies and brokers;
- electoral registers;
- population census material;
- professional directories.

3. Checking a target of study through his connections and contacts

- The case officer or illegal makes unconscious use of his neutral cover connections and contacts to collect information and cross-check individual facts or biographical data about the target of study;
- the carrying out of analogous work using agents and co-opted collaborators of Soviet nationality, and also in isolated cases case officers' wives. The specific task and methods of carrying it out must have been carefully planned beforehand for these people.

In all cases where connections and contacts are used for checking it is essential to be extremely careful and to have a well thought-out cover-story for the conversations in order to conceal the real reasons for our interest in the target of study.

4. Checks in which only Residency officials or illegals take part

- By instigating checks at places of work and residencies of the object of study by means of personal visits or with the aid of the telephone;

- Arranging for surveillance to be placed on the object of study to check his pattern of work; to identify the places he visits, discover his contacts etc. The implementation of such measures in relation to agents must inevitably be combined with tasks which have been specially worked out for them and which will permit the monitoring of their actions;
- The mounting of counter-surveillance on the object of study on previously stipulated routes or routes we know he uses, with the object of discovering any signs that he is under surveillance by hostile special services;
- The use of various operational-technical aids to check agents (will be treated below).

5. Checks through an analysis of the intelligence received
The following considerations must be taken into account when arranging and implementing such checks:

- It is essential to analyse not only the contents of the material but also the nature of the documents – whether originals or copies. First and foremost, measures must be taken to amplify and cross-check data about the sources, the times and circumstances of the acquisition of the intelligence; also a comparison of the material may be made alongside past and other original documents from the corresponding institution, checking typewriter prints etc;
- Side by side with a regular evaluation of the importance and authenticity of individual items of intelligence it is essential to assess the subject's intelligence work as a whole over a specific period of time (a quarter, half-year, full year etc), as this will enable a survey to be made of the overall value of the information and its trends, and will also establish more accurately which of the material from the source is not corroborated by the further course of events.

6. Checking an agent by the imposition of special tasks

The following variants may be considered as examples of the diversity of checks which are possible under this heading:

- Setting the agent the task of collecting basic information and character data on a number of people about whom we already have sufficiently full and reliable knowledge;
- The checking or collection of information on events, facts and

personalities, partly or completely fictitious (if there is no suspicion of possible links between the agent and hostile special services);
- The obtaining of information (documentary or de visu), already well known to the Centre from other sources;
- Preparing for the agent a task which it is outside his competence to fulfil without recourse to specialists or to counter-intelligence (if he is in contact with it). For example:

a)   To visit restricted areas and collect data on such targets as can only be correctly described by someone having specialist knowledge and practical skills;
b)   To send him to a country which has difficult operating conditions to meet a 'valuable agent' within a tight time limit, provided that local conditions make this practically impossible to accomplish without the help of special organs;

- The imposition of a test assignment which forces the adversary to perform specific actions thereby exposing himself to monitoring from our side, for example:

a)   To carry out a check on a specific person in order to collect information about him (places of work and residence, hours of work, the routes he follows, places he frequents etc), an analysis of which must lead the adversary to suspect that we intend to re-establish a lost contact with him and subsequently to organize surveillance in case of a possible change in the status of this person;
b)   To ensure the departure by air of an undercover agent from the country in possession of valuable material (possibility of supplementary checks on the aircraft flight in question or delaying the aircraft);

- the imposition of tasks whose fulfilment would involve matters of principle which the agent would not be able to decide by himself without consultations with hostile special services (assuming he is in contact with them) and this would show itself in his conduct and reaction to such assignments.

An indispensable condition for the successful use of this method of checking is that the tasks should appear natural, realistic, well thought-out, and should flow from the whole course of previous work with the agent.

II. Checking with the help of agents

When using agents for preparing and carrying out checks on targets of study, the following basic requirements must be rigorously observed:

1. Do not allow one agent to be aware of others;
2. The target under scrutiny must not discover the measures being taken by the Residency for checking him;
3. The agent to whom the checking is entrusted must be reliable.

The following are possible options in the use of agents for checking purposes:

- Collecting information about the target of study about his life, business and social activity, contacts, political views, personal and business qualities, intelligence potential etc and also for cross-checking individual facts or events from his life and activities;
- Acquiring specific information from parallel agents enabling material obtained from the person under study to be cross-checked;
- Setting a reliable and experienced agent to study and check the person under scrutiny;
- Organizing surveillance or counter-surveillance on the person under scrutiny;
- Carrying out a secret search of his quarters;
- 'Recruiting' the target of study into another intelligence service with the help of the checking agent;
- Obtaining reliable data on the target of study by means of agents working in hostile Intelligence or Counter-Intelligence Services;
- The utilization of agent facilities to mount the operational-technical measures listed below.

III. Checking with the help of operational-technical methods

1. Checking by means of postal correspondence

- By sending to the address of the person under study a series of letters (a minimum of 5 or 6) from third countries and also from other cities in the country of residence;
- By putting test-letters directly into the post-box in the person's quarters or place of work with all the necessary stamps provided by the Centre together with various characteristics for detecting if it has been opened, including a chemical substance to detect the appearance of fingerprints on the enclosure;
- The object of study forwards his reports using test SW [secret

writing] copying paper (pseudo copy) treated specially for checking against a possible [hostile] chemical analysis with the object of establishing the composition of the SW including attempts to cut off small strips for such an analysis.

It is essential to adhere to the following operational-technical requirements in preparing test-letters:

- The form of the letter must exactly conform to the usage of the country in question (envelope, paper, style of address, quantity, type and value of postage stamps, correct lay-out etc);
- The open text must correspond to the operational cover story for the correspondence and the distinguishing marks on the envelope; it must be written and spelt correctly in whatever language is used. When doing the text of the letter, avoid the use of registered typewriters;
- in selecting an address for reply, it is more suitable to use actual and existing addresses where it is difficult to find the sender (institutes, schools, communal dwelling-houses, pensions, tourist centres etc);
- test-letters must not be kept longer than the period agreed with the 14th Department of the First Chief Directorate as in excess of this time the characteristics incorporated to detect unsealing will make it impossible to conduct a qualitative analysis.

2. Checking by means of test containers and packets
This can be done by sending the person under study to the area for which a cover story has been prepared in order to receive or despatch test containers simulating the arrival (or despatch) of important intelligence material from or to a 'valuable source', using different left-luggage lockers (at airports, railway stations, bus stations etc).

In this case the operation itself may be carried out as follows:

a) the container is placed by a case officer, trusted agent or illegal and a receipt (or key) subsequently forwarded to the address of the person under examination so that the latter may withdraw the container and forward it to the case officer;
b) the container is placed by the case officer, trusted agent or illegal and the receipt (key) transmitted to the person being checked by means of DLB or by personal contact with the case officer (without previously notifying him of the location of the DLB or of the left-luggage locker);
c) the object of study is entrusted with a container to be placed by him

in a left-luggage locker and the receipt (key) in a DLB which will subsequently be emptied by the object of study himself or by the case officer under the pretext of a 'hitch' in the operation involving the arrival of a 'valuable agent' to effect the despatch.

Another method of checking is the use of the residence (dacha, garage, office, etc) belonging to the person under examination for 'storing' test containers (packets) for fixed periods for supposed despatch to 'a valuable agent' who will come to collect the packet under previously arranged conditions of contact. The operation permits of two variants:

a) the object of study returns the packet to the case officer on the expiry of the stipulated period on the instructions of the latter;
b) the packet is collected by another case officer or co-opted person in the guise of a foreigner with due regard for essential security measures ensuring that the checking operation is not blown if the person under study is in contact with hostile special services.

The residence (dacha, place of work) of the object of study may be used for the 'reception' of test containers (packets) from 'a valuable agent' in accordance with agreed contacting conditions and their subsequent despatch to a case officer. The delivery of the container is carried out by another case officer or co-opted person adopting the necessary security measures to avoid blowing the checking operation and to avoid the launching of provocation measures against us in the event that the object of study is in contact with hostile special services.

The object of study can be despatched to an area (airports, railway stations, seaports, restricted areas, other countries etc) for which a cover story has been prepared for a meeting with 'a valuable agent' in order to 'receive or despatch' test containers (packets) as outlined below:

a) the person under study goes for a meeting which is 'aborted' for 'objective' reasons, with the subsequent return of the container to the case officer;
b) a meeting is arranged between the object of study and another case officer or co-opted person in the guise of a foreigner; the necessary security precautions are observed in order to exclude the possibility of blowing the fact that it is a checking operation in case the object of study is in contact with hostile special services.

The object of study can be despatched to a cover area for which a cover-story has been prepared for the reception or despatch of test containers by means of a DLB as outlined below:

a) The DLBs are filled by a case officer, trusted agent or illegal and cleared by the person under study at a pre-arranged signal (without his being informed in advance about the position of the DLB);

b) The DLB is filled by the object of study but then the operation is subsequently cancelled due to the non-arrival of a 'valuable agent', with the container then being collected by the target himself or the case officer.

In the latter case it is essential to provide the person under study with a convincing cover-story to avoid revealing to him the fact that it is a test operation (in case of possible links between him and hostile special services).

When arranging verification measures using test containers (packets) one must bear in mind that these may be carried out with the help of a great diversity of special aids, chemical, photographic and mechanical, which permit a high degree of reliability in establishing whether a container has been opened, whether there has been contact with the contents, whether separate elements have been moved, checks made for SW, or enclosures substituted, whether there are fingerprints or the container and contents have been exposed to X-rays. As regards the last-named it must be borne in mind that special services are now equipped with special X-ray devices (to obtain an image by means of individual impulses) which do not involve exposing any films packed in the container or erasing any magnetically recorded messages.

Additionally when drawing up plans for, and putting into effect, this type of test operation the following operational requirements must be observed:

– The cover-story, the nature and choice of place where the check takes place must flow in a logical sequence from work previously undertaken with the target so as to convince him of the continuity of the proposed operational ploy;

– The containers used must, both with regard to their contents and the camouflage employed, fit into the cover-story;

– The verification operation itself must relate closely to agent-operational conditions and specific events, so as to convince the target of study and the special services (in a double-agent case) that the operation is a genuine operational one;

- The duration of the check must be planned in such a way that the special services (taking into account the technical and operational facilities at their disposal), would be able without undue haste to unseal the container, study the contents and return it to its original condition;
- In order to obtain positive results in checking the target of study by means of this type of operation it is essential to think in terms of carrying out more than one (a minimum of five or six).

3. *Checks with covert code-letter devices*
This involves all the checking in the section on 'Checks by means of test containers and packets', with only this difference, that within the latter one or other of the 'Z' devices [recording apparatus or concealed microphone] is camouflaged.

- The object of study is despatched to an area with a suitable cover-story to fulfil an 'assignment' in maintaining a non-personal contact with a 'valuable agent' (the receipt or despatch of intelligence; giving a pre-arranged radio signal etc) with simultaneous monitoring of his actions from the moment that he is provided with the technical equipment for the operation;
- The installation, with the help of a case-officer or of a trusted agent, or 'Z' equipment [recording apparatus or microphone] in the target's flat or at his place of work or at the place where he is due to meet a person of interest to Soviet intelligence (for the purpose of handing over of a 'souvenir', the transmission of an object for temporary use or for retention, or for a secret identification, etc.);
- The person under examination may be utilized for surveillance or counter-surveillance operations, with simultaneous monitoring of his actions with the help of operational-technical equipment provided for him supposedly so as to transmit previously agreed signals while fulfilling his assignment;
- Or he can be provided with operational equipment for 'recording' conversations of interest to us (at a meeting with a specific person or when visitors call on a colleague, etc.), with simultaneous monitoring of his actions the whole time the checking measure continues;
- The object of study can also be sent to an area with a suitable cover story to fulfil a 'mission' to take air samples to establish the level of radiation, with simultaneous monitoring of his actions from the moment he takes over the equipment;
- Use can be made of operational technical equipment permanently

available to agents (signalling apparatus, devices for the reception or transmission of intelligence, long-distance radio contact etc), or they can be supplied to the target so that checks can be conducted in the course of their exchange under appropriate pretexts (repair, servicing, new model etc) for new items which open the way to necessary monitoring or disclosure of interest in them on the part of the person under examination or on the part of hostile special services.

In selecting this or that method of checking with the help of 'Z' equipment, the following must be borne in mind:

1. The options outlined above are far from exhausting the possible uses of operational technical equipment in checking out targets;
2. When carrying out test measures using 'Z' equipment, all the basic rules for checking objects of study through test containers and packets (precautionary measures and operational requirements for mounting checking operations) remain equally in force;
3. Every checking measure mounted with the assistance of 'Z' equipment requires certain additional preparatory work:

– Preliminary operational-technical reconnaissance with the object of working out a detailed operational plan (the selection and checking of the scenes of the operations, case officer's meeting with the person under study, counter-surveillance and control point, the routes to be taken by all participants etc);
– Certain operational-technical factors affecting the correct choice of the 'Z' equipment must be considered (the timing and duration of the operation, the effects of climatic conditions and other limiting factors, the monitoring of the ether, architectural peculiarities, etc). The task of preparing the equipment must also be studied;
– The serviceability of the equipment and its suitability for the job in hand should be checked and tested in the residency.

4. *Checking with the help of other operational-technical means*
This can be done by:

– Fingerprint analysis of personal reports from the object of study, – either handed to the case officer in the course of meetings or in reports transmitted by post in the form of secret writing;
– The use of special chemical methods for testing the object of study's meeting place with a 'valuable agent' or the DLB (the contents themselves are not treated), the case officer being able subsequently

to establish (at a meeting after the operation) by means of certain devices whether the object of study actually visited the area (assuming that surveillance or counter-surveillance was not possible);

– Sending to the agent, who maintains long-distance one-way radio contact with the Centre, a partially garbled cipher telegram containing a specific task (to go to a rendezvous, or a meeting with a 'valuable agent', to clear a DLB etc) with subsequent monitoring of the object of study's performance, the aim being to establish any possible involvement of hostile special services ('providing' help in the deciphering);

– The use of search techniques for checking the target's car (it is taken from the latter under the pretext of carrying out a meeting with a 'valuable agent') in order to detect any eavesdropping devices, any special fluorescent marks for surveillance of the car by ultra-violet rays, any radio-active marking or radio beacons (checking for plants);

– The use of the facilities of operational points for intercepting the radio communications of the surveillance service to carry out checking measures on agents and illegals in order to detect any signs of the possibility of their being under study by hostile special services (movements on specific routes with strict adherence to time-schedules; going to controlled meeting-places and rendezvous points; clearing false DLBs, etc).

IV. Checking by means of agent-combinations

An agent-combination for checking an object of study is a complex of interrelated agent-operational measures, brought together as a single operational concept designed to achieve an effective test of the object of study.

Agent-combinations may be implemented in a great variety of ways using all the methods of verification outlined above and any combination of these methods depending on the requirements related to the verification of the target, the facilities of the Residency, the characteristics of the specific case, the conditions prevailing for agent-operational assignments in the particular country and certain other factors. In this connection we do not consider it appropriate to give specific examples of possible agent-combination options in the present instructional résumé.

The Centre was also seriously concerned by the danger of Western intelligence operations against the growing number of Soviet trucks and lorries travelling to the West. Much of its fear of 'provocation operations' against Soviet lorry-drivers simply reflected the KGB's exaggerated suspicions of the West. It was easy for conspiracy theorists within the Centre to interpret 'suspicious contacts' and various mishaps on Western roads as part of an organized plot.

The Centre also had, however, one more substantial reason for fearing interest in Soviet vehicles by Western security services. A small but significant percentage of lorries from the Soviet bloc contained sophisticated surveillance equipment. In 1986 a Soviet semi-trailer parked on a minor road near defence installations in Southern Sweden was spotted by local lorry-drivers who devised a method for 'accidentally' removing its tarpaulin cover. Inside they discovered five men and extensive electronic monitoring equipment. Soviet trucks were also regularly observed monitoring tests at the US White Sands Missile Range in New Mexico close to the Mexican border. According to Major-General J.M. Bunyard, project director for the Patriot air-defence missile: 'Every time there is a missile test at White Sands, the vans with telemetry intercept equipment roll right up to the border'.[40]

No 332
Top Secret
Copy No 1

No 8285/KR
30.04.85

Representatives and Residents
(as listed)

MEASURES TO IMPROVE COUNTER-INTELLIGENCE WORK IN ROAD
TRANSPORT ESTABLISHMENTS

Road transport is playing an ever-increasing part in promoting the country's social and economic development and improving the defence capability of the Soviet state.

It carries a great volume of internal and international transport of freight and passengers and in certain parts of the country, it is the main link in the transport system. Road transport is widely used for carrying military freight, raw materials and special products of the defence branches of industry. Information about the location and the nature of production of important defence and military installations and material relating to mobilization matters are concentrated in road transport combines, directorates and enterprises.

The volume of freight transported by 'Sovtransavto' vehicles in West European countries and some states in the Near East has increased in recent years and movement of transport by road has been initiated between the USSR and the PRC.

The special services of the imperialist states and of the PRC display considerable interest in road transport facilities and are stepping up their efforts to gather data which reveal the function and capabilities of the country's vehicle fleet at a time of emergency.

The activity of foreign intelligence services in regard to international road communications has increased. The procedure relating to the time spent by 'Sovtransavto' employees abroad has been tightened up and instances of hostile treatment and recruitment attempts, as well as various kinds of provocation operations have become more frequent. The adversary is exploiting for subversive purposes the particular conditions of 'Sovtransavto' drivers' periods spent abroad, their repeated visits to the same country, and lack of communication with Soviet institutions abroad, and their constant contacts with foreigners, including police, customs and frontier service officers and representatives of firms.

In view of this, the heads of our department are giving serious consideration to the question of ensuring the security of road transport.

One of the latest instructions on this point notes, in particular, that in spite of the measures taken lately to step up counter-intelligence work on road transport, there are still serious shortcomings and omissions in organizing and implementing it.

The steps taken to expose hostile agents have been ineffective and executed without due regard for the specific direction of the adversary's efforts and the forms and methods of subversive activity.

Inadequate use is made of means of preventing the occurence of exceptional incidents and when these are investigated, thorough

research is not carried out in all cases where there is possible involvement of agents of the adversary's special services and hostile elements.

According to the instructions from the leadership of the Department,
the following steps must be taken:

- step up work on obtaining information about the designs and
  subversive activity of the special services, anti-Soviet centres and
  organizations abroad in relation to road transport facilities;
- prepare and carry out measures to plant agents from among the
  drivers and other employees of 'Sovtransavto' on hostile intelligence services with the aim of initiating double-agent ploys and
  drawing away their efforts into channels which are controlled by
  our department;
- take the necessary steps to expose and prevent hostile operations by
  an adversary conducting subversive activity through international
  road transport. Ensure that an efficient watch is kept on the
  operational situation to see how it develops on autoroutes abroad
  and at points where loading operations are carried out, and other
  places frequented by drivers abroad, and react promptly to any
  change in the situation by organizing intelligence counter-measures
  in this direction;
- prepare and carry out measures to compromise the special services
  and their agents engaged in hostile cultivation of Soviet drivers,
  inducing them to betray the Motherland, creating opportunities for
  recruitment and mounting provocation operations;
- carry out more thorough processing of foreigners who establish
  suspicious contacts with members of Soviet vehicle crews, in order
  to find out if they are involved with foreign special services;
- arrange for systematic exchange of information with the friends
  [other Soviet Bloc Intelligence Services] on the organization of
  counter-intelligence work on international road transport, and also
  about the discovery of the adversary's efforts, directed against
  international road transport and recruitment approaches to drivers
  from the USSR and other socialist countries. Plan and execute
  measures to study foreign road transport firms belonging to
  capitalist states, through which the hostile intelligence services are
  operating, and anti-Soviet centres and organizations abroad, and
  take steps to put a stop to their subversive operations.

Please keep us regularly informed about what action the Residency takes to improve intelligence and counter-intelligence activity in international motor transport.

In particular, please examine the Residency's agent and other resources for dealing with these tasks and include the necessary action in the year's plan for the lines concerned.

Please report not less than once a year on the adversary's hostile activity against road transport targets, as part of the report on the operational situation in international road communications, as envisaged by guideline No 2314/KR of 23.2.84.

VADIMOV
[V.V. KIRPICHENKO]
[First Deputy Head, FCD]

The Threat from the 'Main Adversary'

The main strategic priority of FCD counter-intelligence during the decade before Gorbachev came to power remained 'the struggle against the subversive intelligence activities of the American special services'. The plan for 'intensifying' counter-intelligence against the Main Adversary in the period 1983–87 gave 'a particular emphasis' to 'measures to combat enemy ideological sabotage'. The Centre interpreted Zionist support for Jewish refuseniks, nationalist agitation in the Baltic Republics, 'ideological warfare' against the Soviet Union and plans 'to undermine the Soviet economy' as part of a subversive master-plan co-ordinated by American Intelligence.

[ms notes: Incoming 27
Comrade Gornov, Yelin, Brown
and operational staff of the   Copy No 1
Residency
Leonov
26.1.84
Yermakov [A.Y. Guk]

No 84/KR   To Residents (personally)
06.01.84   as listed

PLAN FOR BASIC MEASURES TO STEP UP STILL FURTHER THE EFFORT TO COMBAT THE SUBVERSIVE INTELLIGENCE ACTIVITIES OF THE UNITED STATES SPECIAL [INTELLIGENCE] SERVICES

In circumstances where the United States special services are continually increasing their subversive intelligence activities against the USSR and expanding the scale on which hostile methods are used to undermine the military and economic potential, defence capability and preparedness for mobilization of our country, it is essential, in the interests of safeguarding state security, that the counter-intelligence service abroad should take steps to increase its counter-measures against the adversary to a substantial extent, and improve still further the level and effectiveness of our action against American intelligence in all sectors of the struggle.

In October 1983, the heads of our Department accordingly put into operation a 'Plan of basic counter-intelligence measures for intensifying to a greater degree the struggle against the subversive intelligence activities of the American special services in the period 1983–1987'.

The following tasks have been set for Residencies in accordance with this Plan:

- gathering information about the aggressive plans and designs of ruling circles in the USA and its special services, with all available help provided by our resources, in order to implement Soviet foreign and domestic policies;
- uncovering and preventing American special services' intelligence activity, particularly when using agents, against the USSR, reliable protection for Soviet state, military and other secrets, and defence of the Soviet economy from adversary wrecking and sabotage;
- putting a decisive stop to acts of ideological sabotage on the part of subversive centres and organizations abroad operating under the control of the American special services, and ensuring the security of Soviet institutions and citizens abroad ...

[ms notes:] Astakhov   16.2.84
James   9.02
                                                          Fedin
Gordon   8.11
                                                Artyom 9.2.84
Evans   [illeg name] 9.2.84

One of the main sections of the Plan envisages making the maximum use of existing agent and operational facilities in Residencies in order to obtain intelligence on the following items:

- signs of preparation by the ruling circles in the USA for a nuclear attack on the USSR, and any measures they take designed to weaken our country's defence capability, or to create focal points of tension in various parts of the world;

- specific plans of the American special services for agent penetration of Soviet state and military secrets and eventual training and infiltration of agents into our country in order to carry out diversionary sabotage operations;
- the adversary plans and actions to undermine the Soviet economy, or commercial and economic, scientific and technical co-operation between the USSR and other countries;
- operations planned by the American special services and centres of ideological sabotage associated with them and designed to step up psychological warfare' against the USSR, with the aim of discrediting our foreign and domestic policy and undermining the Soviet state and social system.

In order to extend existing operational facilities for obtaining reliable data on the efforts, and forms and methods used in agent activity by the American special services, and for taking steps to uncover this promptly and put a stop to it, Residencies must complete the recruiting action already approved in regard to members of the American special services and proceed to organize fresh targets to process for recruitment.

The Plan has in view a series of additional measures aimed at penetrating the American intelligence service's agent network from third countries' territory.

A particular place in the Plan is occupied by measures to combat the adversary ideological sabotage. In response to the tasks confronting our Service in this important sector of counter-intelligence work, Residencies must take specific steps to pursue more energetic study of centres belonging to anti-Soviet émigré and Zionist organizations abroad, which are utilized by hostile special services for subversive operations against the USSR and Soviet citizens abroad.

The Plan also envisages suitable additional measures to be taken to reinforce physical security and technical protection of Soviet institutions in the USA, and in a number of countries where there is a difficult counter-intelligence regime and an unstable operational situation. In order to counteract attempts at recruitment and other hostile activities by the adversary against Soviet citizens serving in posts abroad,

Residencies must continually improve their counter-intelligence methods for working in the Soviet colony and its environs, making the fullest possible use for this purpose of agents and other operational assets in the special services and state institutions of the USA and third countries, and also official contacts of security officers with representatives of local authorities. At the same time, Residencies must take care to improve the standard of preventive work carried out among groups of Soviet citizens abroad.

Progress in carrying out the measures envisaged by the Plan must appear in the Residencies' annual reports on the work of the counter-intelligence service abroad.*

You and your deputy for 'KR' [counter-intelligence] matters must personally familiarize yourselves with the Plan in the Centre (Comrade Vladimirov's subsection), utilizing for this purpose a visit during your next leave.

ALEKSEEV

[GRUSHKO]

[next page]
For Comrade Gornov [Gordievsky]
Lavrov [Nikitenko] 22.VI.84

Though The Centre's conspiracy theories about American sub-version became somewhat less extravagant during the later 1980s, they did not disappear. In the nine months before the abortive coup of August 1991, the KGB leadership voiced public fears of Western plots to infect Soviet grain imports and des-tabilize both the Soviet Union and the Soviet economy.[41] In June 1991, the First Deputy Head of the FCD, General Vadim Vasilye-vich Kirpichenko, (whose codename 'Vadimov' appears on a number of documents in this volume) complained publicly that 'the recent outburst of glasnost' and 'transformations in the USSR' were assisting an intensified 'CIA offensive against the Soviet Union'. Despite Kirpichenko's disclaimer, it was clear that the United States remained the KGB's 'Main Adversary'.

VADIM KIRPICHENKO ON AMERICAN ESPIONAGE (Novosti Press Release, 5 June 1991)

'It is harder for Soviet secret agents to operate in the United States than

---

* This paragraph is underlined and sidelined, with 'Yermakov' written in the margin

for their American counterparts to work here', asserted Lieutenant-General Vadim Kirpichenko, First Deputy Head of the KGB's Foreign Political Intelligence Department [FCD], in an interview with Novosti's Vladimir Ostrovsky.

General Kirpichenko referred to the greater openness of Soviet society, its profound democratization and the recent outburst of glasnost, and to new factors which are making the tasks of foreign secret agents easier to fulfil. The intelligence officer believes that the transformations in the USSR have in particular created conditions that make it easier for Western secret agents to establish contacts with Soviet citizens.

The General also thinks that such radical changes have not occurred in American society. Consequently Soviet secret agents find it just as hard to operate now in the USA as they did in the past.

As before quite influential circles and specialist bodies systematically create spy hysteria campaigns for domestic opinion. The American press constantly publishes material about the work of the KGB, its intelligence service, etc. Kirpichenko noted that such a campaign clearly maintains the heightened sense of concern the American public feels about national security.

Referring to the work of the CIA, the General drew attention to the way employees of this agency go flat out to obtain information from those Soviet citizens who have access to state secrets. He went on: 'We notice that Soviet citizens abroad are approached by CIA agents and other special services. Many of them are simply offered the chance of staying in the USA or working for the CIA. At times such proposals are made at random to strangers on the street.'

Kirpichenko called this a CIA offensive against the Soviet Union. He believes that such a campaign has two aims: on the one hand to obtain secret information cheaply and on the other to reduce the activity of Soviet secret agents by intimidating them through encroachments on Soviet citizens.

The General singled out the following assessment from a recent (16 May 1991) report of the US Defence Intelligence Agency (DIA) to Congress's Joint Committee on Economics: 'Despite the political, economic and ethnic crises, the USSR remains a single country, capable of delivering a mortal blow to the USA.'

The General considers the publication in the American press of such information to be planned with the sole aim of putting pressure on the Soviet leadership. This conclusion is supported by certain indirect evidence: a year ago in London a secret group of experts – intelligence section heads – was founded and had a single aim: 'to regularly devise assessments, which will pressurize the Soviet leadership into doing something'.

Kirpichenko continued:

> We could take as one example of the activity of the secret services their attempts to influence public opinion on the problem of Soviet–Japanese relations. They also disseminated misinformation about our alleged readiness to cede the islands in exchange for a large provision of credit from Japan, and other rumours.
>
> At the same time, foreign intelligence services' interest in gathering data on the Soviet defence and science and technological potential, our reserves of strategic raw materials, foodstuffs, hard currency and gold has also increased perceptibly.
>
> We are well aware that American secret service agents have increased quite significantly over the past few years the number of trips they make to the Soviet Union. This activity would seem to confirm the axiom that on-site reconnaissance remains as vital as before.
>
> However, electronic intelligence has provided the major part of information for the US through numerous tracking stations, surveillance of Soviet telephone communications and satellite interception of radio messages.

The Soviet General emphasized that the degree of technical sophistication of special services is being constantly upgraded, in particular, CIA's liaison techniques which are highly advanced. According to Kirpichenko, US intelligence is invariably perfecting its techniques and forms of activity. Almost every year, Soviet state security bodies come across new methods of activity conducted by foreign intelligence services.

Speaking about Robert Gates' appointment,* the Soviet General recalled the words of this newly nominated US expert on Soviet affairs: 'Discrediting the KGB's past and present activity may seriously affect its prestige, undermine its personnel's morale, and thus serve to expand the sphere of activity of US intelligence in the Soviet Union.'

It should be mentioned in this connection, Kirpichenko observed, that on more than one occasion the Soviet leaders stated that the USSR

---

* the nomination of Robert Gates to succeed William Webster as Director of Central Intelligence (DCI).

does not regard the United States as its adversary, while the US administration has not made a similar statement to this effect. This circumstance is of special importance now, and, regrettably, it serves to fuel hostile stereotypes of the Soviet Union among Americans.

In the aftermath of the failed coup of August 1991, the traditional KGB assessment of the threat from the 'Main Adversary' was publicly ridiculed even by some KGB officers. The FCD was accused by one of its officers of having 'profaned the essence of intelligence work'. 'We served mainly Party interests', he told *Izvestia*. 'To please our bosses, we passed on doctored and slanted information, in accordance with the slogan "Pin everything on the Americans, and everything will be OK". That's not intelligence, it's self-deception.'[42]

Ironically, soon after the August coup, the newly appointed head of the KGB Analytical Directorate, Vladimir Arsentyevich Rubanov, pointed to the United States intelligence community as the main model for the reorganization of the KGB.[43] In October 1991 the First Chief Directorate was hived off from the restructured KGB to become an independent foreign intelligence agency, and given a name curiously similar to that of its traditional main opponent: the Central Intelligence Service.

Notes

Abbreviations:
KGB   Christopher Andrew and Oleg Gordievsky, *KGB: The Inside Story of its Foreign Operations from Lenin to Gorbachev* (London: Hodder & Stoughton, 1990).
Instructions from the Centre: Christopher Andrew and Oleg Gordievsky (eds.), *Instructions from the Centre: Top Secret Files on KGB Foreign Operations, 1975–1985* (London: Hodder & Stoughton, 1991).
Unless otherwise stated, the source for information on the KGB and its foreign operations is Oleg Gordievsky.

1. *KGB*, pp. 487–507. *Instructions from The Centre*, Ch. 4.
2. Jeffrey T. Richelson, *The US Intelligence Community* (Cambridge, MA: Ballinger, 1985), pp. 35–41. Desmond Ball, 'The Development of the SIOP, 1960–1983', in Desmond Ball and Jeffrey T. Richelson (eds.), *Strategic Nuclear Targeting* (Ithaca, NY: Cornell University Press, 1986).
3. The expansion of S & T (scientific and technological intelligence) collection increased the overlap between KGB and GRU operations. There also appears to be an enormous duplication of effort in sigint between the two agencies. KGB, pp. 510–11.
4. Vitali Vasilyevich Fedorchuk, KGB Chairman from May to December 1982, was not a Politburo member.
5. Gordievsky
6. *KGB*, pp. 372–3.
7. Erich Honecker, *Zur aktuellen Fragen unserer Innen– und Aussenpolitik nach dem IX. Parteitag* (Berlin, 1976), pp. 13–14. We are grateful to Professor Jefferson Adams for this reference.
8. Arkadi N. Shevchenko, *Breaking With Moscow* (New York: Ballantine Books, 1985), pp. 224–5.
9. Friedrich Thelen, 'Post-Cold War Spies: Cloak and Stagger?', *European Affairs*, May–June, 1991.
10. Peter R. Prifti, *Socialist Albania since 1944; Domestic and Foreign Developments* (Cambridge, MA: MIT Press, 1978), Ch. 12.
11. Ibid., pp. 253–5.
12. Gordievsky
13. *KGB*, pp. 484–7, 536–7.
14. *KGB*, pp. 473–5.
15. *KGB*, pp. 475–8.
16. *KGB*, pp. 512–13.
17. *KGB*, pp. 477–8.
18. *KGB*, pp. 463–5.
19. Gordievsky
20. *Instructions from The Centre*, Ch. 9.
21. *KGB*, pp. 461–2.
22. Gordievsky
23. *KGB*, p. 463. Gerald Segal, 'The Soviet Union and Korea', in Gerald Segal (ed.), *The Soviet Union in East Asia* (London: Heinemann, 1983).
24. *Instructions from The Centre*, Ch. 1.
25. *KGB*, pp. 411–17.

26. Kuzichkin was posted to the section of the Second Department which prepared documentation and 'legends' for illegals in Turkey, Iran and Saudi Arabia.
27. Vladimir Kuzichkin, *Inside the KGB* (London: André Deutsch, 1990), p. 105.
28. Two less important, long-serving KGB agents, Ali Naghi Rabbani, a senior official in the Ministry of Education, and the retired General Darahshani were also caught in 1977–78. Ibid., pp. 147–8, 197–9, 222.
29. Ibid., pp. 298–303, 365.
30. *KGB*, pp. 458–9.
31. Gordievsky. For further discussion of KGB operations in the Middle East, see *KGB*, pp. 455–61, 530–1.
32. *KGB*, pp. 342–8.
33. Gordievsky. The anti-Masonic dimension of Zamoisky's conspiracy theory is elaborated in L. Zamoysky [*sic*], *Behind the Facade of the Masonic Temple* (Moscow: Progress Publishers, 1989). The antisemitic dimension was considered unsuitable for publication.
34. Geoffrey Hosking, *A History of the Soviet Union* (London: Fontana, 1985), pp. 438–9.
35. *Instructions from The Centre*, Ch. 1.
36. Gordievsky was clear that the Plan was not simply, or mainly, a response to Israel's intervention in Lebanon in June 1982.
37. *KGB*, pp. 10–12.
38. *KGB*, pp. 142–4.
39. On the vast KGB and GRU sigint operations since the 1960s see *KGB*, pp. 437–42, 510–12, and Desmond Ball, *Soviet Signals Intelligence (Sigint)*, Canberra Papers on Strategy and Defence, no. 47 (Canberra: Australian National University, 1989).
40. Desmond Ball, 'Soviet Signals Intelligence: Vehicular Systems and Operations', *Intelligence and National Security*, Vol. 4, No. 1 (1989).
41. *Instructions from The Centre*, Ch. 10.
42. *Izvestia*, 25 Sept. 1991.
43. *Izvestia*, 18 Sept. 1991.